Creativity, Teaching, and Natural Inspiration

Interwoven Adventure Stories, Teaching Stories, and Memorable Magical Moments

A nonfiction work by Mark A. Doherty

Creativity, Teaching, and Natural Inspiration

Interwoven Adventure Stories, Teaching Stories, and Memorable Magical Moments

A nonfiction work by Mark A. Doherty

Creativity, Teaching, and Natural Inspiration

First Edition Paperback.
Published by Unsolicited Press
www.unsolicitedpress.com

Cover Art: Kathryn Gerhardt
Editor: Analieze Cervantes

The author has tried to recreate events, locales and conversations from his memories of them. In order to maintain their anonymity in some instances the author may have changed the names of individuals and places, identifying characteristics and details such as physical properties, occupations and places of residence.

For information, contact the publisher at
info@unsolicitedpress.com

Unsolicited Press Books are distributed to the trade by Ingram.

Printed in the United States of America.

ISBN: 978-1-950730-02-5

Contents

Creativity, Teaching, and Natural Inspiration

Interwoven Adventure Stories, Teaching Stories, and Memorable Magical Moments

A nonfiction work by Mark A. Doherty

Prologue

I am the smoke from a driftwood fire, spiraling skyward among the stars, or dissipating at dawn into the early dew. I am the spark, the flame, the ember of creativity, touching the senses in myriad ways. My energy diffuses through all walks of life, stark or subtle, tempestuous or calm, tangible or intuitive; like smoke, I permeate the senses and work my magic upon the world.

"Students, today's journal entry is *Something I Dream of Doing*." As a fifth-grade teacher, Mrs. Blake turns writing this title in her *click slide* chalk whisper of cursive blackboard, I already know. I want to climb Mt. Everest.

"If you could do anything when you grow up, what would it be?" asks ninth grade grammar guru Mr. Rothberg. Two sharp hand claps shout directions, "Describe it. Write it." Three quick finger snaps add, "No—Sentence—Fragments." I miss the last part because I'm already sailing around the world.

"What do you *want* to write? What are you *good* at writing?" Inquires high school history storyteller, Tom Shaw. I look past his Navajo rug style vest and ponytail to see my own novel, floating like an eagle feather in the air above him.

This is a story of a teacher, yet it is also a story of a life. It is the life of a boy who dreamed of climbing Mt. Everest, of sailing the world's oceans, of writing the great novel, and later of performing music on a national concert stage. Lovely dreams they were, like soft ice cream cones on a summer's day. Yet that boy never accomplished any of those particular dreams. He did something twice as hard—

he became a teacher. I am that boy, now sixty years old, but my childhood passions still beckon like the distant cry of a Redtail hawk, and throughout those wonderful years between boyhood and today, I did climb and ski and sail and kayak and write and perform music and spend nearly as many nights out under the stars as I spent days in front of my students. Enhanced by imagination and creative thought, my mountains became taller, rivers swifter, lakes vaster, and unpeopled lands became a wilderness. The same was true of the physical objects, both natural and man-made, that I found along the pathways of my many journeys. Maybe that's why I use a wheelbarrow full of funky objects—stuff I've collected from the journey of life—when I teach English and writing. Maybe that's why I take my students into eddies on our great river trip of learning and we all bob around like driftwood or message-carrying bottles encircled by stories, songs, and great memories.

"What happens," I ask my students, "when your boat goes into an eddy?"

"You sink?" comes a reply from speak-first-think-later Jake. Everyone chuckles.

"Possibly, if you don't enter the eddy right, or if it's a monstrous eddy. What else?"

"You spin around," offers a more thoughtful answer from Heather.

"Ah, yes, and what general direction do you go, let's say, if you keep from spinning too much?" But I don't wait for this answer. Instead, I walk down between two rows of desks, take a turn, spin around once, and then begin walking the opposite direction, gesturing the downstream water away with my hands.

"Welcome to The Eddy, students. When you drop into this classroom from the river of students moving down the hall, you eddy out. And frequently you, me, and everyone else in this room, this eddy, will even go upstream against the current."

My first days in the classroom followed a thirteen-year stint as an outdoor guide, musician, free-lance writer, and odd-jobber. Suddenly I found myself indoors—every day, all day. Furthermore, I found myself faced with ordinary tools—grammar books, literary textbooks, curriculum guides—to be used for teaching something extraordinary: language and writing. I also found myself tasked with teaching largely reluctant learners—high schoolers who cared more about friends and cars and going places than English and writing. For a moment, I considered returning to the low pay, hard-edged, competitive world of guiding and music, but I'd invested some time and money returning to school to obtain a teaching certificate. I went to work, stepping out of the fresh air and into the noisy walls. In order to survive, I brought the outdoors, the creative spark, the music, and poetry with me. Here's how it all evolved.

Chapter 1: Ponderosa, Sing to Me

Of all the writing topics I employ, the one closest to my own heart is simply a chunk of firewood. It came, indeed, right straight from the firewood pile. Of course, it's been fixed up a little. I first cut it down to the size of a three-inch wide wheel, sanded one side, put some varnish on it, and made a little stand to hold it upright, the concentric rings facing out. To explain my personal attachment to this hunk of wood, I must first relate a pre-teaching memory.

I lean against the great tree, bark crackling against my shoulder, close my eyes and listen. Wind whispers through the needle-y limbs of the massive branch-heavy ponderosa pine. My wandering memories flow back to the blue Colorado sunshine and the tree-clad foothills of my youth. I breathe the pine-scented air and begin to remember. Wind streams through the boughs, and I hear the stories told by the pines. Their sighing voices speak of such things as climes, and soils, and open glades through which wanderers have walked for hundreds of years. They sing for ecology, and they talk to humanity. As the breeze rises like water, the great trees also tell much of my own story.

The voice of the ponderosa can be heard throughout the West—its stately form as distinctive as great elk bugling in a meadow. The geographical pattern designating its regions of growth, when plotted on a map, is as imaginatively complex and unique as its reddish brown and gray bark. The places the ponderosa pine graces range from hills and valleys to lake shores, from river canyon gorges to mountain slopes, and from Mexico to Canada, California to Colorado. Any place within these broad boundaries, where perfect soil chemistry mixes with a not quite desert aridity, you'll find this majestic, resplendent giant.

Pines are marvelous teachers; from them I have learned history, culture, ecology, art, and even how to work. Let's begin with the four to nine-inch needles, dark green, bunched in threes, which are the perfect length for Native American basket weavers. They are not too short like the bristlecone, pinyon, or lodgepole pines. They are not so thin as the sugar or Norway, not as fat as the limber or white-bark pines. They are just the right length, breadth, and consistency, familiar to the weaving hand—as familiar as the Latin name of *Pinus ponderosa.* Much of this I learned when my mother became enamored of Native American crafts and began weaving her own pine needle baskets. They were soft yet strong, pliable yet stout. And when freshly made, they carried the essence of pine in both color and scent. Could a human personality emulate that of a pine needle basket?

The wind flows like a river in the pines, and the aroma of sap and cones and bark and pollen and new growth candles brings a flood of other memories—and more knowledge.

The ponderosas were my childhood friends, for they were wonderful trees to climb, to rest in the shade beneath, to wander through. An open forest floor of soft, rebounding needles and duff often held ponderosa's companions—mushrooms, pine drop plants, and wild current. And the fox and the blue jay and the tufted-eared black squirrel always watched as I played. It is such places that foster creativity and wonder that lasts a lifetime.

Later on, however, I learned of yellow mistletoe, pine bark beetles, and the blights that affected second-growth timber. And so, I also learned about cutting dead trees and harvesting firewood. Due to their slow-to-moderate growth rates, the ponderosa wood is dense, thick with resinous, rich smelling and sticky sap, and the wood burns hot and long. The size of this tree's limbs, which make huge knots, and the pitch-laden density of this pine's wood make firewood sized rounds impossible to split—nearly. There was no Robert Frost style of "squarely hit" and "splinterless blocks" and "ax poised aloft." No, ponderosa wood laughed hysterically at an ax, and then it ate it with such tenacious jaws that sometimes one had to burn the entire log before retrieving (and replacing the handle of) the ax. Ponderosa logs had to be split with a fifteen-pound sledgehammer and steel wedges. In hard-earning my spending money, I hardened my muscles, my splitting technique, and my work ethic. Many years later my father built a homemade log splitter, but not before we split by hand ten years' worth of our family's winter wood, and as many loads to sell for my allowance.

Yet nothing takes me back to the memory of cutting firewood more quickly than the sweetly acrid smell of pine. If you could turn turpentine into an elixir similar to the Stone Pine liquor of the Alps, you might imagine the sweet strong smell of Ponderosa sawdust and split wood. It takes working with something as powerfully pungent as pine sawdust and splinters to imbue into one's essence the power of the olfactory senses. Want a pure memory? Smell it.

Firewood was the first use I understood for ponderosa, but the sighing boughs told other stories, and soon I learned to listen, to feel, and even to smell those stories. Those other stories begin with the witness tree. The veteran ponderosa pine could live for nearly a thousand years. Only the bristlecone, Sequoia, and whitebark pines live longer. Therefore, the ponderosa oft became the chronicler of history, of routes and trails throughout the West, of boundaries to property, and claims to gold. Many aged veteran trees with bark furrowed inches deep, limbs as large as smaller trees, and treetops leveling out in an almost African Baobab tree profile would bear a foot-long, deep scar carved through the thick bark into the sappy yellowish-white wood beneath. These "blazes" as they were called would mark trails and routes, property corners, and mining claims—often even numbers were carved into the wood. Frequently, the ponderosa witness tree was the telltale sign of ancient mining roads, ghost town foundations, or overgrown and caved in gold mines throughout the West. I learned to imagine what else the tree had witnessed. Did it see Brett Harte's John Oakhurst, the honest gambler, pin his ace to a ponderosa before unloading his Derringer as one of the "Outcasts of Poker Flat"? Did it watch the wagons travel West dreaming of gold? Was it once a hanging tree? So much can be imagined, and so for me, a great tree like a ponderosa was always a witness to the passing ages. They taught me to love the story.

We've all seen some of this history in old film. The ranch in the classic television series *Bonanza* was named "The Ponderosa." Acting stars from musicals to western movies traveled ponderosa lined trails over hills of ponderosa and stayed in cabins built of ponderosa. Settlements and towns were set in ponderosa forests, and characters were buried beneath great reaching limbs of ponderosa pines. Glued to the television as a youth, I reveled in the stories. Bored by the television as an adult, I marvel at the film records of magnificent and healthy historical ponderosa forests. I watch reruns for the tree shots.

With mining came milling of wood, and the ponderosa pine became the beam, the brace, the siding, and the winter heat for many mining towns. The only trees to survive the harvest were those growing in cemeteries and on inaccessible slopes. Hills were denuded by the needs of the gold rush. This wood was stout and strong, and so it also became the twelve by twelve timbers that shored the hard rock tunnels underground. It became the ties to secure the mine rails in the tunnels and the narrow-gauge rails clinging to the mountainside. The high trestles spanning the deep gorges were often built of great pine beams. It also became the mine shaft trestles rising high into the sky like primitive oil derricks which housed the mine shaft hoists. And Ponderosa was used for the huge mills and the hanging sluices that brought water and ore to the machines for processing. Nearly a hundred years after the mining boom, as a boy, I could still walk on solid timbers of mine engineering where the structures remained so solid that their ancient creaking was less loud than the protesting calls of my worried parents. But the built-to-last mines and towns had a much larger and lasting impact, and that was, and still is, the impact of second growth timber.

Therefore, the singing of these great trees transformed into the throaty humming and ringing of a giant, six-foot diameter steel saw blade of my father's sawmill. The river of wind in the trees was interrupted by the roar of the great diesel engine of a homespun sawmill, brought back to life from the ashes of an earlier era. So prolific were these trees that from the late 1800s until the late 1900s, they grew back over denuded hills into a deep green forest, punctuated by tall specimens of veteran trees— those spared by the original cutting. They grew more thickly than the old forest, and there were fewer fires to thin them out, for fires destroyed homes and mankind began putting the fires out. Nature found a new way of thinning the forest—the pine bark beetle.

My father began cutting dead trees from his thirty-five hilly acres when I was just a boy, but by the time I was a teen, the pine bark beetle disease process had accelerated, and Dad needed help. Taking some time from his government job as a geophysics researcher and electronics engineer, he joined with a local shop teacher and a local builder, found an ancient ruined sawmill in a nearby nearly ghost town, hauled it home, and the three rebuilt it. I helped. The plan: make lumber out of all that dead wood. The dead and dying ponderosas that were destined to sing no more now fell to my raucous chainsaw. But when the coughing saw sputtered to a stop, and the whining winch finished its truckload, I would still hear trees singing in the wind—many of them great veterans with the sap and strength to "pitch out" the boring beetles. And I would always eat my cucumber, onion, and hard salami sandwich beneath some giant surviving ponderosa and reverently watch its great boughs play with the sunlight and shadows.

But that's where this story ends and the story of the sawmill begins, and that is a tale for another time. Whenever I see a ponderosa pine forest, I listen to those stories and hear the winds in the back of my mind. I think of walking through those widely spaced giants with their sweet-smelling reddish bark, massive limbs reaching skyward with sometimes a thousand years of tales to tell. I place a hand on a great bole of one tree and ask it to take me back again to where the wind whispers in the boughs and the warm sun paints a thousand pictures on the pine-needled soft forest floor upon which I rest my imagination and so many of my memories.

Sometimes I think of life as a great quilt, each story being a square of intricacy and creative detail and hand-sewn care—part of a life's fabric, drawn warmly over to comfort the sleeping memories. Many of those memories reawakened when I began teaching, although I could never fully impart to my students, for instance, the powerful impact the smell of fresh-cut pine held over my emotions. I could only impart to them that smell, the olfactory sense, was one of those elements of sensory imagery that had a certain quality which evoked memories more powerfully than any other of the five senses. Woodsmoke is another trigger. Each time the scent reaches me, lucid memory floods my mind like the river in springtime. More importantly, smoke elicits creative thought. Certainly, this is one of the secrets of incense in ancient cultures. Smoldering sage as well guided the metaphysical journey of America's First People.

I still use that same hunk of firewood as my second writing topic of the year, and lessons surrounding it continue evolving. Teaching is all about making connections, and connections are all about concrete understanding. I can lecture all day long, blowing wind through the didactic forests of words, but thumping my knuckles on a piece of wood, then passing it around for students to touch, to feel, so smell—well, it makes ideas more solid, like a piece of hardwood furniture. That polished up hunk of spruce firewood, like all the objects I employ in teaching, puts a bit of concrete into the abstract. Within a week or so, I move to a new object, but I always look back at the wood chunk and think about how many more teaching ideas reside in lessons built around this wonderful object—built around almost any object. Someday using the wood topic I'll move into the realm of the great cedars of the Northwest and First People's culture of wood—so much potential. Writing topics—polished, worn, held by a thousand hands, they remain in their battered boxes waiting to spill ideas into students' notebooks. Like folk songs, we sing them to life year after year.

Chapter 2: Feathered Friends

"Look, look, there's an Eagle!" I exclaimed. Everybody looked up from the Anasazi granary our group was admiring. As a guide, I prided myself in knowing not only the sights but also the wildlife.

"Awk, awk," came the sound from the soaring bird above us.

Awkwardly, I confessed, "Sorry, false alarm. It's a raven." Nature has a way of keeping us humble. Eagles have a way of changing into ravens just to ensure that guide hubris never gets out of hand.

But ravens are incredibly smart, and useful in their own right in the wild ego-driven world of the back-country guide. Their distinctive call is unmistakable; their personality is always amusing. If one is savvy, that raven personality can work as an ally for the creative backcountry guide, which reminds me of mountain bike tour.

I was more than happy to be driving the sag wagon that day, with fellow guide Danny on the mountain bike herding the group of twelve troubled youth and two counselors on up the Southern Utah desert trail past Monitor and Merrimack Buttes to the highway and then down to the canyon below Gemini Bridges for our evening's camp.

Moby Dick, my old Ford F150 was loaded to the gills with water, food, camp kitchen, and bicycle camping gear. After cleaning up lunch and watching the riders depart, I had three precious hours to myself. Boy, were those kids a handful! I wondered if a trip like this would turn any of them around, or just set more firmly their resolve to be jerks. But guiding pay was guiding pay, and we took the trips that came along. Plus, I got an extra $100 per day for employing my own truck as sag wagon support vehicle. And there were moments of alone time, like this one after lunch when the truck had to navigate a road route by itself rather than the narrow, single track bike trail the group would ride. These moments were nice.

By the time we hooked back up, herded the crew to a few viewpoints and an old cattle trough for a refreshing splash, it was time to camp. I was refreshed from the time alone and ready again to deal with the clients.

Dinner went off reasonably well. Few complaints come from hungry cyclists, even if they are teenagers. But after dinner, as the sun went down and we lit a campfire on our environmentally friendly fire pans, the kids seemed restless. *Playing sing-along-songs on the banjo won't cut it with this crowd* I thought to myself. *I think it's time to punt!* And so, as dusk fell like a giant cloak down in the canyon, I decided to try my hand at a good old-fashioned ghost story. After all, the canyon bottom was eerie and shadowy and much darker than it would have been up on the rim. The silhouettes of the rocks were taking on ghostly forms themselves. The setting was certainly prime, why not? So, I called the group together.

"Hey, gather round. Something everyone needs to hear! Attention, come, come!"

Danny and his designated helper looked over from their dish duty. He seemed puzzled but relieved that someone was redirecting the teenagers' attention for a little while.

When the noisy group finally settled around the fire, I began. I had to make up the names, but the story began with a factual event, one that we'd told them about earlier in the day as they approached the cliffy views at Gemini Bridges. Of course, all we said then was, "Be careful. Last year one boy fell to his death here. They couldn't even get the body out until the next day. What a mess!"

I began: "It was on a night just like this one, exactly one year ago to the day, that Joey Blaine died up here in this canyon. His brother Billy had jumped the gap between the twin arches, and then he told Joey to try it. Joey leaped, got one foot on the far rock, then fell to his stomach. Slowly it seemed, he slid back towards the void, one hand reaching desperately for his brother, and then he vanished right before Billy's horrified eyes and reaching hand. There was a moment of extreme silence, and then Billy heard a sickening thud come from the canyon bottom. Yep. That was a full year ago, and believe it or not, I hear people in town tell some pretty spooky stories about that death and this particular canyon. They say that on nights like these, queer things sometimes take place up there by the twin arches where Joey met his fate."

A few of the youth were now listening intently huddled around the flickering campfire as I spoke. A few others turned slightly away with classic "I don't really care" body language nonetheless cast furtive glances at the dark high cliff walls silhouetted by a starlit sky.

Seeing one of them glance at the walls above, I took a cue and resumed. "Way up on those dark and forbidding walls, folks have seen things at night sometimes that they just don't want to talk about. Makes 'em nervous about camping here. Makes it easy for us to get this site. They come back to town sometimes with looks on their faces that would make the sunniest day pale and remind us all of just how black and dark a deep canyon like this can get in the middle of a night like this."

"Oh, oh, I can't stand stuff like this. Stop!" Exclaimed one girl with her face wrinkled, her nose ring dancing about erratically.

"He's just full of it. Stupid jerk stuff. I'm goin' bed!" huffed a tough looking black-haired youth with several spindly chin hairs mimicking a beard sticking out of his jaw. He then scraped the dirt as he rose and stomped off towards his tent several yards from the fire.

I exchanged meaningful glances with the group leader counselors who were in charge of the dozen or so troubled teens before them. Earlier one of them had told me, "I've got to warn you, some of them are a bit rude, don't care for anyone but themselves. So don't be offended by anything they say or do. We just need to be sure they are not causing direct physical harm to anyone."

Watching the teenager walk away, I spontaneously called after him, "The last person to walk away from the fire alone on a night like this was the first to see what some say is Joey Blaine's ghost, so watch out!"

"See what? Your stupid face making up stories?" Came the sarcastic reply as the boy hesitated just past the last of the light cast by the fire.

"See for yourself. But tonight's one year to the day since it happened. In fact," I said turning back to my remaining and now very rapt audience, "it's one year to almost the hour since one of the rescuers, working his way in the dark down a rope to try recovering the body saw a sight that changed his life forever!"

An angry zipping of a tent door momentarily eclipsed the crackling fire as the youngster flopped into his tent. I noted the sound and shifted my ammo can seat slightly around so that my voice would carry to the tent in the darkness.

"He had just reached the lower end of his one hundred and fifty-foot rappel when he heard a weird sound. He pulled up hard on his figure-eight descending ring and peered down into the darkness. Blaine was lying grotesquely deformed on the rocks, head cocked sideways, but his eyes were open wide, just like he was alive and awake, and they were staring straight ahead at a ring of seven of the largest black ravens anyone has ever seen! The rescuer let out a yelp of surprise as he caught the gleam of the ravens' eyes and then jerked his head back to look at Blaine. Starting to get really scared, he was about to call up to the men on top who were now asking him what was up when he noticed that the ravens had vanished. They had disappeared without a trace, without so much as a whisper of wings, without so much as even a scraping of claw on sandstone. Then the rescuer noticed that Blaine's eyes were nothing but two empty sockets, dark and ugly, nothing there, eyeballs suddenly vanished.

"Whoa, that's too weird!" exclaimed another one of the boys still sitting around the fire.

"Gross, no eyes?" commented one of the girls.

"Ah yes, no eyeballs. The coroner said later that the impact of the fall had popped them out. But the rescuer swore otherwise, and he's been back here since a few times to try to find out the secret. His rope didn't reach that night, so he jumared back up. You kids know how long it takes to climb up a vertical rope with ascenders, right? Imagine, every time that rescuer rested and looked down, Joey's empty eye sockets stared back up at him. But he went back for the body recovery the next day.

I heard movement in the nearby tent as I continued.

"And he was up here just last month, on the eleven-month anniversary, right where that tent over there is, camping in his own tent alone when something really strange took place."

Everyone moved a little closer to the fire, all eyes peering in the direction of the tent where the obstinate boy had gone. There was a pause, and only the crackling of the fire could be heard.

It was working, this story, so I added with emphasis: "And while he was in his tent, he opened his eyes up and *there was one of the very same huge black ravens* standing right in front of him *inside his tent!!* It shook its head at him, and dropped *a huge, blood-stained, glassy eyeball, right at the foot of his sleeping bag!"*

Collectively the group moaned and made several sounds of disgust and fright, and at the same moment, the zipper on the wayward tent zinged open at a speed that might have melted the interlocking teeth. Just as the teenager stood up and faced the fire, I shouted out "Listen, Listen, everyone!" If what I thought I heard was right, this would be a perfect addition to the story.

My voice echoed twice in the canyon, for I had shouted over the general melee of the kids, then put a finger to my lips and said, "Shhhhhhh, listen!" Silence momentarily prevailed. But within seconds a new sound came from high up on the canyon walls. It was the sound of a raven calling, and it echoed through the canyon and fell upon the startled faces of the listeners. A chill ran down my spine as I wondered how some darned old raven would happen to fly by and croak a few times *right on cue*! Weird.

"Exactly one year ago," I whispered, "and kids, personally, I'm not in much of a mind to stay up in *this* canyon tonight. But that's how the trip was planned, and there's nowhere else close that's good to camp. And tonight's the *Twelve*-month anniversary! I wouldn't be surprised to see a ring of ravens on that rim sometime soon, and I damned sure wouldn't go wandering about in the dark tonight!

And that was it for my story inspiration. The night was still young, the fire strong, and all I had left was the old banjo. So, I took it out and strummed a few tunes, and by the end of the evening I had most of the kids singing along, forgetting that they wore chips on their shoulders, yet maybe not forgetting about the spirits in the night, the stories of the canyons, and the magic. The next day everyone seemed to get along famously.

Now every time I see ravens, I think of my impromptu story and wonder how impromptu the lone raven's visit really was. As a creative muse for teaching, the raven remains.

The feather of a Sandhill Crane lay beneath a great cottonwood tree along the creek next to the field that was bisected by a paved walking trail. I happened to notice the feather one crisp October morning while walking from the parking lot to school where I was fulfilling my long-term substitute teaching assignment working with a cantankerous fifth-grade class. I picked up the feather and carried it to school, placed it safely hidden on a high shelf top, and began my last day ever of teaching fifth grade. A phone call at lunch informed me that a contract position, take-it-or-leave-it-right-now, was offered at the high school. My job with the fifth-graders would end as soon as their permanent teacher recovered in a few months. The high school job was potentially permanent.

"But I've just got these fifth graders under control," I said to the district office secretary. "Can't we make the switch at first quarter?"

"School board wants the change now. If you don't want it, we'll take our second candidate."

So, I left Moab, Utah's Helen M. Knight Elementary that day, carrying only my satchel and my newfound crane feather and headed to our town's Grand County High School. The next day a vice principal stated coldly, "Come with me, we're going to assign your classes. School board has mandated that we cut the class size in our English courses."

He marched me into the classrooms of three different English teachers, 9th, 10^{th,} and 11th grades, and read names from a list. Then he stated flatly: "You students have a new English teacher, Mr. Doherty. You need to follow him to . . ." and he for each class he listed one of four different destinations. "Get your things and go with him now." The school didn't have enough rooms—I was also to become a roving English teacher. Not one of those students or teachers knew it was coming; neither did I. When I got home that night, Deborah, my companion of three years, took me down to the river.

"You look like hell. What happened today?"

It was October, the water was cold. I took the plunge. When I finished wiping the muddy Colorado from my eyes, I looked up and saw an eagle (yes, this time it was the real thing) soaring along the rim above Castle Valley. I remembered the crane feather, dipped it into the inkwell of my creative mind, and prepared to embark on a teaching odyssey that would last these twenty-seven years and is still unfolding. I took that feather to the *new* school the next Monday, and I began my program I called "Daily Writing." It was an idea I dreamed up years earlier when I first considered teaching English and contemplated ideas for getting students to practice different types of writing.

How does one make the abstract more concrete? I asked myself.

Well, bring something concrete into the room, and write about it, came an answer while on a long desert hike.

From there I searched for a plan to match the five-day school week. A few miles down the trail, I came up with the idea: Mondays—informative writing, Tuesdays—

technical writing, Wednesdays—poetry, Thursdays—creative prose, and Fridays—dialogue. A piece of firewood, for instance, would be a great topic. After all, at one point in time wood comprised the schoolhouse, desks, pencils, paper, books, and even the warmth from the stove in the schoolhouse. *Yes,* I thought to myself with a smile, *wood would be good, but what should the very first topic object be?*

The answer came when I found that feather. That long, slender brown Sandhill Crane feather followed me from class to class that first week. It rode on top of the roll-y cart they supplied me with for roaming from room to room. I've seen many other new hires over the years push that damned cart around; not many of them ever stuck with the job. It was a clumsy, awkward time for both me and my new students, most of whom were 11th graders. But when we started talking about feathers, at least for a few magical moments, all else was forgotten.

"Why might a feather make a good first-day writing topic for us?" I ask.

"Because it's cool," Cheerleader Mary replies.

"Indians liked them," Charles, who thinks himself cultured, chimes in.

Then I hold the feather up from its shaft, bend over a desk, and pretend to write. "Now what do you think?"

"You can use them to write with, like John Henry!" Jonathan exclaims from the back row. "Somebody said he had a really neat signature."

Right concept, wrong era. I am planning on beginning with the transcendentalists in Junior English. *Maybe I'd better go back to the Declaration,* I think. *After all, our national bird is the eagle.* "I think you mean John Hancock, one of those signers of The Declaration of Independence. You can see a picture of his signature on page 23 of our textbook,"

I lift the book up and flash the photo of the yellowed document and walk across the front rows, letting everyone ogle over the signature. "It's also on the wall in front of the main office. And yes, it's a nice signature, but what's more amazing is that he did it with a feather shaft dipped in ink." I'm hoping that the feather object lesson will enhance the reading and writing lessons I will soon be employing to teach the English 11 core curriculum as it blends American history and literature in a mostly chronological order, beginning with the Puritans and the Patriots.

I return to the front of the room, put the textbook down, take up the chalk and continue, "Ok, so let's brainstorm about feathers. Day one of this object-oriented writing process is all about communicating common knowledge—let's call it informative writing. I want you to compose a page discussing in general the merits of feathers. For instance, what can you make out of feathers? First, let's write down pens. A feather pen is called a quill."

"How about pillows?" volunteers Suzanne, the girl who still carries stuffed animals with her books. Now we're rolling. Before long, the list has grown feather dusters, coats, sleeping bags, arrow fletching, bookmarks, and more.

"Hey, I know, *decoration*, like Peacock feathers in a vase," chimes in Jennifer, our resident art lover.

"Whatever tickles your fancy," I reply. Everyone looks puzzled. I add, "That idea is really a feather in your cap, Jennifer." Still puzzled. "Metaphors, anyone? Write these down: birds of a feather . . . lightweight boxers are called. . . tapered edges . . . don't get upset or don't get your feathers . . . and by the time we hit ruffled feathers, it's time to move on to feathers in stories, songs, books, fantasy worlds. We finish with a general discussion of the scientific study of feathers, flight, and birds. Before I turn them loose to write a page, I seize the opportunity to compare Josh's tie-dyed brilliant attire with Megan's modest brown sweater and grey slacks. "So why does the male bird always have the brightest plumage?"

The next day we discuss the feather in detail, microscopic barbules and all, and I get to introduce words like *aerodynamic* and *resilient.* By day three, we've thought a lot about feathers and all but forgotten the awkward remixing of classes. We might even have enough ideas flying around in our minds to create a poem on day three. Nonetheless, I always start with a simple example:

A Journey
These soft
Yet interesting things
Are fun to play with.
They are part of a bid,
And yet they can do so much more.
Imagine a feather
As it makes its way
From a bird
Into a
Pillow.

by Mr. Doherty

The poem, and all that came before it, really warms us up for prose writing on day four, so I include a few simple instructions as well as some sample starts. It goes as follows:

Write two pages of creative prose using a feather or feathers for your idea or point of departure. Copy at least one of these starters:

As the snow began to fall outside, John stoked the fire once more, then reached for his great quill pen and began to write. The tip of the feather danced in the firelight as he wrote about . . .

There it was, a huge goose on the lawn, and our hacky-sack had landed right in front of it. My girlfriend (boyfriend) looked at me as if to say . . .

I'll never forget the day I found an eagle feather on the ground. At first, I didn't think it was really an eagle feather. Who would expect such a special feather to be. . .

Finally, for the closing of this writing topic, the feather day five, I introduce our fictitious classmates Fred and Sally, explain that they will be with us all year and that our job on day five of each writing topic is to transcribe their rather quirky and sometimes comical discussions. I'm always amused at the looks on students' faces when I ask for five to ten paragraphs of writing here. Were it not for the classic conventions of writing dialogue, this *would* be a daunting task:

Copy this dialogue start and write seven more paragraphs of dialogue:

Sally looked over at Fred and asked, "Hey Fred, any guesses what Mr. Doherty will have for the next writing topic?"

Fred replied, "I guess whatever tickles his fancy."

"Good feather joke, Fred," Sally responded poking him in the arm. "No really, what do you think it will be?"

On Friday, the feather acquires a prominent display spot in the classroom where it can wiggle in the breeze as students walk past it and it continues to tease their imaginations. By the end of the year, the whole wheelbarrow of stuff will adorn the top of the bookshelf, all spent writing topics simmering on the back burners of our minds. These items include a chunk of fossilized ripple rock, a carved fish in a fishing net, some rope made of yucca blades, an antique iron, a hand-braided bullwhip, several pieces of climbing rope, seashells and tide tables, old mukluks, a leather Huck Finn style hat, a 1960's transistor multiband radio, some garage-sale *Canadian Flyer* figure skates, a pair of wooden cross-country skis (they hang over the edges of the wheelbarrow a bit), a 1939 birding guide, a 1929 Grammar School English Pamphlet series, a forest service arrow trail marker sign, some deer antlers, a round wheel of firewood, and bag of Anasazi chert flakes, but the feather always rises above.

Chapter 3: The Sound Calls All Souls to the Fire

Bleached and smooth, the old driftwood curves around the rocks and sand. It has literally been carved by the waters' hands—first tossed, then torn, and then worn by the river as it traveled the flowing miles. I pick up this work of nature's art from the stones of the river passing by and placed it upon my evening fire. I wonder. And as the smoke rises it dissipates into the starry night sky, melding with the Milky Way where Cygnus and Aquila glide next to Lyra—the summer triangle. In the coals of the fire I see stars, and in the burning stars, I see glowing embers. Another wisp of smoke pierces my memory, another song comes to mind, and I pick up the old five-string banjo and start to play. The sound calls all souls to the fire—the burnt-out river guides finishing dinner cleanup, the disoriented river trip tourists processing their first night outdoors without streetlights or subways, and all the other campers mellowing into a night on the river. It was more of a selfish interest that made me switch from the acoustic guitar to the banjo for the preferred camping entertainment implement. Simply stated, nobody gets a few cocktails in them and asks to borrow one's five-string banjo like they do a guitar, and nobody has to endure bad singing and worse playing until the guitar can be pried from their ego-charged hands. But serendipity took over, and I soon realized that the banjo, mostly plastic and metal, made a great spare paddle in emergencies, didn't fall apart when a boat flipped and had a certain echo that rang across the water and off the canyon walls that makes people smile and sing along. It had its time and place, filling the gaps between the silence and sounds of nature right at the moment nature loomed largely and seemed too much.

One thing it never did, however, was rival the song of the canyon wren.

As the melody of that uniquely American instrument lingers in my mind, so does another story from the canyons, from the river.

It was going to rain, there was no doubt about it. Any over-hopeful thoughts that the thunderstorm might miss us were quickly dispelled by several bolts of lightning and a cool moist change in the evening breeze. Almost before the echoing thunder finished reverberating from the deep canyon walls of the Colorado River, the guests grabbed their picnic plates of fried chicken, potatoes, and a brownie, and then they scurried onto their dry tour bus. They left behind bedraggled river guides to clean up dinner in the rain and load up the boats and gear from the evening float trip onto the waiting gear trucks and trailers.

But I was neither one of these tourists, nor one of the guides. I was also not one of the truck drivers, nor the tour bus driver. No, I had been paid a small sum to drive out to the evening float trip takeout dinner beach and to play a few songs while the guests, mostly Europeans, ate their dinner. The plan was for this to become a form of a modern Kokopelli's Café, which was ostensibly giving guests time to reminisce on their fun-filled evening of rapids, swimming, and scenery, before heading to their next western tour destination. The music was planned also to give the guides some extra time to lay out the pre-cooked dinner and to even load boats and gear before it got pitch dark. Then at dusk, with the guests full and content, all would exchange smiles, handshakes, and of course tips, before departing forever.

Things were not, however, going as planned. It was now raining—hard—and I stood in my poncho holding an old five-string banjo wondering if the tour company would pay me if no-one stayed to listen to songs. The banjo was tonight's instrument of choice. It was mostly waterproof, echoed nicely off canyon walls, carried well with noisy groups, was a pure-blooded American instrument, and was always a hit with Europeans.

Suddenly I realized that I was actually sweating in my poncho, for the rain was not really cold. It was actually refreshing, cool, and sweet after the near hundred-degree day we'd had. I shed my poncho as the rain let up to a gentle shower of sparkling raindrops, making the sand and sage and river smells come alive in a pungent bouquet of olfactory delight. A little rain wasn't going to hurt the old 5-String, and so I thought I might as well play a few tunes for the guides as they humped the heavy rafts and gear up the wet sandy beach to the waiting trucks.

Maybe all that river-soaked humanity eating on the tour bus got stuffy and hot, or maybe someone else realized that summer rain in the desert is something to be stood in and savored rather than avoided. Either way, the result was that a few of the European tourists trickled back out into the rain to listen, to smell, and to just be part of a fragrantly moist and beautiful desert evening.

I kept playing, and before long a couple more tourists came out, and soon after a circle began to form, and then like the rainbow that was glimmering up canyon beneath the translucent edges of the storm, I noticed that voices began to sing along.

It's hard to say when the entire bus emptied, or when the guides finished their work and joined the circle, but by the time darkness fell, seventy people from as many as a dozen different countries were holding hands in a huge circle, swaying side to side like waves on the water, all singing together.

The songs they were singing became the most magical part of the entire evening. There is a type of song that transcends time, race, religion, personality—a type of song that is known in at least five languages—a type of song "folk" sing when they gather. These are songs like Kumbaya, My Bonnie Lies Over the Ocean, Michael Row Your Boat Ashore, Today, Let There Be Peace on Earth, and many more. They are songs that seem to have been written for everyone and can be sung by anyone. That night, by the Colorado River, beneath the sweet air of a summer thunderstorm, the stars witnessed a picture of human beings from many *different* walks of life doing something like *one*, together, in harmony—it was a singing cultural rainbow.

The tour group was scheduled to return to their motel by nine but didn't make it until at least eleven. The guides forgot about the next morning's early float that many would have to rig for after getting back. The musician forgot about sore fingers and sang until his voice started to wear out. The river flowed inexorably on towards the sea, and time saw the evening end, but for me, and I would imagine many others, this particular event is timeless. I moved on from guiding, rivers, and performing music. But I carry with me a picture of multicultural bliss which is a glimpse into one of the scintillating possibilities for our world. Tips that night for both me and the guides were great, but we all knew that something that transcended tips had occurred. I carry with me a hope, inspired by such moments, that someday humankind will evolve spiritually to a place where we always stand and sing, swaying in harmony with each other and with the beauty of the natural world.

It took me many years to fully integrate acoustic music into the high school classroom, but it took only moments to see how the acoustic guitar and lyrical song could capture the attention of even the rowdiest class and hold them for a few moments. I started using old popular and folk-style songs in English class whenever there was a link to a unit, a topic, an essay or novel or story that we were reading. Joni Mitchell's "Big Yellow Taxi" worked beautifully for introducing Rachel Carson's *Silent Spring*. Amy Ray & Emily Saliers' "Close To Fine" neatly closed John Knowles' *A Separate Peace*. John Denver's "The Eagle and the Hawk" made a wonderful summary for the first writing topic of feathers. Gordon Lightfoot's "Home From the Forest" fit perfectly with Veteran's day and his "Canadian Railroad Trilogy" fit many themes of westward expansion and American literature. Sometimes a song linked directly to the literature we studied; such was the case with "Heart of the Appaloosa" by Fred Small and Chief Joseph's "I Will Fight No More Forever" speech.

At some point in time I realized the basic truth that music and melody is a glass that holds the elixir of poetry, and when students grasp the contents of that glass, they suddenly become intensely thirsty. At another point in time, I intuited that I should *start* each class with a folk song and an accompanying discussion of the poetry. There was no turning back. Artists like John Prine, Kate Wolf, Greg Brown, Paul Simon, Peter Rowan, Mary McCaslin and many more found their home in English class. And kids didn't want to be late, not because they'd lose their starter points, but because they'd miss the song. On some occasions, when the poem merited, we'd extend the discussion long into the class period. As the years passed, I continued to be amazed that just a simple guitar and voice with no extra accompaniment would consistently hold the attention of young people who routinely listened to loud and raucous complexities of full-sounding music. Actually, what they called music I called just noise. *Ah, noise*! I thought to myself one day, *the acoustic folk song, in its own right, is an escape from noise. That's part of why they like it, and they don't even realize this.* I now believe that the simple human voice accompanied by an instrument of wood brings us very close to the natural world as well. And then another tale from my past returns like a forgotten song lyric; it's a story that explains much.

Where do you put old wacked out uranium miners, 3.2 beer alcoholics, and burnt river rats when a busted town goes boom again without them? You put them in a watering hole, a hangout, a hideout, a bar in which they can entertain the feeling of ownership. You put them there, out of the way, just off the beaten path, and let them drink.

What do you name that type of watering hole? How about The Outlaw Saloon. The Outlaw, it was more of a clientele gathering than a specific physical locale. The bar actually moved from a dubious Quonset hut structure to a ramshackle adobe hacienda while I knew it. And when it moved, the drinkers, and the barkeeps, and the musicians moved with it.

But during the early '90's in Moab, uranium miners, old river guides, and 3.2 alkies were seriously displaced by the modern suave, sleek and in-shape post-yuppie mountain biker generation and the business boom their money brought to a hungry little town-gone-bust since the '70's uranium decline.

And there was often friction. Granola eaters versus miners, environmentalists versus ranchers, boatmen versus bicyclists, gearheads, and pinheads versus motorheads, and counterculture health food nuts versus bar counter alkies. As the years now pass, I look back and muse upon the irony that many of these groups now "work together" to battle bigger elements in life than simple lifestyle differences. But back then, the differences were noticeable. Yet the local cops knew that as long as so-and-so was at the outlaw saloon getting beer-logged, they weren't out making other troubles elsewhere. They weren't out bugging the new money-spenders coming into town. That was a good thing.

At first, none of the new sport mountain-bike crowd ventured into such smoke-filled lairs as the Outlaw, but after a while, some of the tougher, braver ones, seeking more of a *real* experience, would chum up to the bar and buy themselves a beer or two. Nobody complained too much—after all, cash speaks the same language everywhere.

And so as the clientele began to mingle a bit, it increased, and the owner sought out a bit more sophisticated live music on the weekends in hopes of drawing crowds while still entertaining the old-timers. She even put a rickety bike rack up next to the Harley parking circle.

That's when I became a part of the sociological experiment, largely by coincidence I might add. Some time back, I had boasted to the local country rock band who were practicing up for a gig at the Outlaw that I could make the five-string banjo sound good to anything they played—rock, blues, swing, etc. After proving this to them during a few living room sessions, four of us, Mike, Cash, Christine and myself, became Desert Skies, a country-rock band, and had a two-to-three night a week job at the Outlaw. Christine washed out during the first weekend due to a fight with Cash, but the three of us guys regrouped and played on for months using a rather eclectic mix of banjo, bass, electric and acoustic guitar, and a fancy drum machine. We played songs ranging from old '60's hits to hardcore country. After a while, I even introduced a couple of mainline bluegrass tunes to boot. "The Ballad of Jed Clampett" from the *Beverly Hillbillies* was one song I truly regretted introducing, so many times did we have to play it, sometimes five times a night.

The beer flowed like the muddy Colorado and the brown bags flashed like lightning and the cigarette smoke billowed thick as the great Yellowstone fires, and there was a fight every night.

It was rough and wild, living up to the name Outlaw. But the money was good, and Deb and I were building our own home in the nearby Castle Valley, which was a full-time day job all by itself. No time for other work during the days, so music on the weekend nights became some bread and butter along with being a field course in humanitarian sociology and the West.

Shortly before the end of my run at the outlaw, a remarkable event took place, one that both Deb and I still talk about. It caused a distinct bump, a skip perhaps, in the sociological experiment we were immersed in at the Outlaw, and yet it was really a rather simple event. A malevolent thunderstorm rumbled through late one Friday at about nine-thirty, passed to the north of town, and one mighty strike of lightning took out all the power to Moab for the entire night.

The bar was packed, the band was tuning, the amplifiers were warming up and the beer was bubbling from the taps. As I set my banjo on its stand, careful not to crimp the cord plugged into its internal microphone, I thought about the hundred plus dollars that I might *not* be earning this night if the band couldn't play. None of us could really afford to take a night off and lose the income, and that's what drove me to think, *The band couldn't play?* Well, couldn't be amplified was more like it. The banjo was acoustic, one of Mike's guitars was acoustic, and Cash's bass, well, *that* was expendable. It was his voice that was his strength anyway. So, I mentioned this to Mike, our band leader. Soon after he smoothly sidled up to the owner who was still pulling beers from the cooler and popping caps by flashlight and made a suggestion. Since the phones still worked, we could call up a couple of other friends who played acoustic guitar and mandolin and we'd do some guitar, banjo, mandolin music on the patio—after all, the beer was still cold, and the cash register was old enough to work manually as well.

She agreed, and more importantly, agreed to pay the band if it worked out. Soon Steve came by with his mandolin, Jerry with his Guild guitar, Mike pulled the plug on his acoustic/electric Yamaha, and I grabbed the trusty old Ode banjo and we began to play. Cash disappeared into a table of women and I don't recall seeing him again, although he came around for the full paycheck when it was all over. We were indeed going to get paid, so I was happy. But what transpired throughout that evening was remarkable, memorable, even inspirational.

To begin with, there was not one fight, not one squabble during the entire night. The angries, the orneries, the crazies, the alkies, and all the others, just sat talking, laughing, and often singing side by side like best buddies. Several times I saw dyed-in-the-wool old miners smiling with granola mountain bikers. Several times I saw old timers who never got along chumming up and talking and toasting. The local police stopped in to check, fearful of what mischief might be transpiring at the Outlaw during such a power failure and they shook their heads in amazement at the harmony of humans, the festive yet incredibly peaceful scene. One said, "No problems here!" and they moved on, not even batting an eye at the liquor being consumed outside on the patio and sidewalks. They didn't seem to mind clusters of politely conversing patrons sipping bottles of brew all the way out into the street. There was a circle of sound in which everything seemed harmonious.

It was as if the acoustic gathering had lifted the guise from everyone there. Pretense was gone with the amplifiers and gentle laughter and relaxed conversation pervaded the air like the scent of rain on sage as the stars shone overhead in the huge desert sky above the isolated lightless town. The cigarettes glowed, the beer flowed, and the notes and harmonies of acoustic instruments and voices washed over everything like a gentle summer's breeze.

It was late when we finally packed up the instruments and headed home beneath the stars. The town's lights were still out, but the lights that existed in the hearts of the people of the Outlaw Saloon that night shone ever so brightly.

So, I return to the lyrical song and the students. I imagine the classic folk song, passed down from old to young, taught by ear by parents to their daughters and their sons. I feel folk songs walking me through memories of days past and gone, reminding me of wars and of heroes and of deeds people have done. The words and the melody rest in my mind, written to speak to all ages, all time, while painting a pictured colored with rhyme. And I sing that folk song now in my own special way, and share it with the young, who I hope will also sing it someday. I imagine the classic 1960's, 1970's, and 1980's songs moving from popular song status into folk song status.

When I sing starter songs for the students, I don't let them applaud. Primarily, I want them to be writing their thoughts and immediate reactions, secondarily, I want a second of pure silence to follow each song. I like to listen for the sound of words falling lightly onto lined pages, it's like listening to snow falling.

The concept of combining poetry and song grew like a sapling in fertile loam after I introduced it to my students; the idea matured in my honors classes. It took me a while, however, to understand why it was so effective. It compelled me to look at the roots of Western verse. Entire generations of American poets and lyricists were raised on classic British and American poetry; they studied it in schools, and some carried it in their back pockets. Walt and Emily had long since broken rules of rhyme, meter, capitalization, and form in poetry. They pioneered new poetic style for American writers. Certain British poets like Blake, Pope, Coleridge, and Shelley also demonstrated effective poems flourishing outside of the classic genres of poetry, but for the most part American lyricists from the 1940's through the 1990's routinely employed classic poetic techniques. The starter song in class was the perfect place for students to identify advanced usage of poetic elements such as metonymy, synecdoche, symbolism, antithesis, advanced rhyme, meter, assonance, consonance, alliteration, irony, and onomatopoeia. Once in a while, a songwriter's lyrics were a bit short, and so I added a verse to these songs, attempting to keep the particular poet's style and form intact. John Denver's "Annie's Song" acquired a third stanza, as did Kenny Loggins' "House at Pooh Corner" as well as Peter Yarrow's "Puff the Magic Dragon." At first, I simply included the "new" stanzas under the original authors' names, but soon my astute students found that Loggins, Yarrow, and a few others had finally added their own new verses to their songs. One day a student brought me Kenny Loggins' new verse added to the end of "House at Pooh Corner" and asked me why the "new" verse I showed them was different. I simply explained that a friend had sent me the verse, and I thought it was Loggins' work, but it must have been my friend's lines. Thereafter I opted for my sidekick, Marc Robertson, to take the responsibility. After all, he was one of our local favorite songwriters who composed during his time numerous songs about the outdoors, and in particular Southern Utah and Colorado—a man after my own heart. (Yes, he *was* my own heart, my own self, but the pen name allowed me to stay in third person whenever presenting poetry, and for more than twenty years, the secret remained with me.) There are many stories revolving around Robertson's musical career. The following story is indeed completely true, but when relating it to students, I found it much easier to slip into the Robertson third person persona.

"One never knows when they will need to write something," I tell my students. "Maybe it's just a note to coworkers, maybe it's a set of directions, maybe it's an essay for school—or maybe it's a poem for someone. Let me tell you a story Marc Robertson once related to the audience one night when I saw him do a concert over in Grand Junction, Colorado.

"During the mid-1980's, Robertson was working at Pack Creek Ranch in southern Utah, wrangling horses by day and waiting tables and playing music by night. One day ranch owner Jane Sleight told Robertson that an out-of-town lawyer recently visited her. The lawyer, replete with suit and briefcase, ostensibly represented music copyright giants ASCAP and BMI and asked if she played on stereo, or if any of her musicians performed any songs copyrighted by these corporate monsters. He then attempted to exact an exorbitant monthly fee so that she could continue to play music as usual—a threat of a lawsuit backed up his demand."

"What did she do?" asks one of my students.

"First she removed all popular music from the cassette tapes next to the restaurant stereo system. She kept out only classical music. Then she asked Robertson if he played any ASCAP or BMI songs, which of course he did, along with his own original music."

"What did *he* do?" comes the next question.

"Well, he promised Jane that he'd play only his own original work; he had plenty of songs. But there was a problem for Robertson. Can you guess what it was?"

"All his songs were the same?"

"Ah, you are close. Think again, what happens when people are listening to a guitarist? What do they often do?"

"Applaud?"

"Yes, if they are listening closely enough and not salivating over their prime rib. And then?"

"They make a request!"

"Bingo. And you can guess that they request well-known songs, and who do you think owns the air rights to many of the well-known songs?" I leave the rhetorical question hanging for just a second. "ASCAP and BMI."

"So what did he do?"

"Well, he started writing new verses to every song he knew from the ASCAP and BMI list, then called himself a co-writer, and kept on playing requests."

"Did the lawyer ever come back?"

"Robertson said that he was never challenged; the lawyer returned once, but Jane Sleight insisted that she was not playing any ASCAP or BMI music, then she explained that *her* lawyer would be available for further discussion. The man never returned after that. It was probably a misguided scam. But it certainly scared many rural restaurant owners for a while. That same "lawyer" made the rounds throughout Western Colorado and Southeast Utah. Robertson told me once that he'd love to have challenged that lawyer, even though his wife said he'd probably lose if it ever came to that. What the whole thing did do was give him lots of extra songwriting practice though. Remember those new verses to "Annie's Song" or "Puff the Magic Dragon" or "House at Pooh Corner?" How about "The Ballad of the Green Berets?" I ask my students.

The digression has lasted long enough. I finish: "But I personally like Robertson's own lyrics best. We'll hear a few more of Robertson's songs later this semester. Now let's get back to our own writing. Today is poetry day, and I'm looking for a fifteen-line poem about . . ."

Telling the Robertson story to students always reminds me of another story, my own story, behind the impetus for writing poetry in the voice, vernacular, and style of other songwriters. It took place before the ASCAP lawyer made his play, but it is important because it gave me the confidence to make my own play in the face of those seemingly false demands that emanate like foul air from authorities, administrators, and other misguided individuals. I sometimes tell this one to students as well, but they hear it as another Marc Robertson tale.

I am playing songs for tips at the local bar. It's winter, down by the tracks in the town of Montrose, Colorado. About three months ago I loaded up the car and drove around the Uncompahgre Plateau from Moab to find work for the winter. There just wasn't any river guide work in Moab during the cold months.

It is 1985. The bar has a television, a stereo, a musician, lights—cell phones are still a dream away. Two people are eating dinner at a nearby table, another three are sitting in the back room conversing over coffee, and two men sit at the bar sipping cocktails. Once in a while, someone nods in my direction at a familiar song or a guitar lick they like, but it's mostly a very quiet evening. My tip jar, which is my only pay besides a ration of two beers per night, holds three dollars and some change.

I'm enjoying the time, though, and I'm playing some songs I rarely play and hardly even remember. "One Tin Soldier" comes to mind and I muddle through it. Then I try to recall a few newer songs that are still being polished. I sing "Home From the Forest" by Gordon Lightfoot, then "Hello in There" by John Prine. I notice one of the older men at the bar looking periodically in my direction. He motions to the barkeep, hands him a note, and remains cemented to his stool staring alternately into the mirror and into his cocktail. The barkeep John walks over to me and hands me a note which reads, "Request: "Song for the Green Berets."

"Wow," I say to John, "That's a good one, and a melody that I certainly remember. But I never memorized the lyrics."

"Charlie knows them, he was a vet also," John comments as he gestures first to the gentleman at the bar and then toward the kitchen behind the bar where another man wearing a short-order cook apron and a rumpled wool cap is slouched on a stool pondering the newspaper. "Why don't you go ask him?"

"Thanks," I reply and put the note in my pocket, set the guitar down, and head for the kitchen. On the way, I stop by the bar and speak to the man who requested the song.

"I'll be back in a minute. I don't recall the words to that song, but I think I know someone who does."

He nods and smiles faintly but says nothing. I move on.

Charlie knows some of it, all of one verse and part of a second verse and a few scattered words from the rest of the song. I scrawl them awkwardly on a napkin. He also knows the songwriters' name, Staff Sergeant Barry Sadler. I thank him and go sit at a table in the empty back room of the café; the coffee-drinking conversational trio has now departed. The nearby public library might help the search engine that is my brain, but it is closed. Many years later I will find online the original version of this song, and also learn that someone named Robin Moore is also credited with penning the poem.

I strum the chords and recall the melody. I think to myself, *Nice song.* Charlie nods approvingly from the kitchen where he's thrown a couple of garlic burgers on the grill—a few more locals are in for an evening snack and a beer. *Wish I had more words . . . can't really do a song on just a verse and a half, can I?* Then another thought comes to me, *Why not write a few more words? It's a super slow night, who cares if I take a half hour to work up a song?*

I sing the chorus one more time, *Fighting soldiers from the sky, /Fearless men who jump and die, /Men who mean just what they say/These are the men of the Green Beret.* Then I ponder the partial verse Charlie provided, *Put silver wings on my son's chest/Make him one of America's best.*

I think about why wings might be placed on his chest. I write *A Mother's son is laid to rest/Grant me this my one request.* I return to the first verse Charlie provided, *Fighting soldiers from the sky/Fearless men who jump and die/Men who mean just what they say/These are men of the Green Beret.* Charlie also recalled the line about only three in a hundred men winning the honor. I wonder what makes a person join the Green Berets, and I write, *From their families and their homes/Here to rise above they've come* and then from Charlie's memory, *100 men will test today/Only three win the Green Beret.* From there, the next verse comes naturally: *Not for honor, pride or shame/Not for fortune or a name/Just to keep their homeland free/They give their lives across the seas.* Now I have a complete song. Not quite the original, but in the same spirit I hope. I rewrite the poem on a larger napkin, then return to my stool in the front room.

After a short apology to barkeep John, Charlie, the two men at the bar and a group of four people waiting for their burgers, I sing the song with my head bent slightly down reading my napkin notes. I repeat the first verse at the end. The man at the bar who requested the song listens without turning in my direction. As I finish, he pushes his empty glass forward, rises, and turns to me. I see tears in his eyes as he walks across the small room and drops a bill into my beer mug tip jar. Then he speaks, "Son, you can't buy memories. Thanks." Then he leaves the bar and I never see him again, except in *my* memory.

About an hour later I finish up. It's nearly ten on a winter's weeknight. The grill and bar are closing. I pull the four bills and change out of my tip jar. There are three wrinkled dollars, some quarters, and one carefully folded hundred-dollar bill.

The starter song lyrics did have their limitations though. There is so much more to teach from the rich history of poetry, especially Western poetry. Sonnets come to mind.

"So what's the point," asks one of my colleagues one fall day, "in teaching sonnets as a part of English? They'll never read them on their own, they'll never write them, and if they aren't in AP English, they'll likely never see one again."

I answer, "Basketball."

"Huh?"

It's the same answer I give to my students when they complain about having to "blueprint" sentences. (I call classic sentence-diagramming –*sentence blueprints*).

"Basketball, and free throw shots." I continue, "learning a sonnet is a mental exercise. It's a practice problem in English just like we use practice problems in math, or like we practice a thousand free throw shots for basketball." My colleague doesn't know that personally, I hate basketball. My depth perception as a youth was limited. I took one too many nose shots, and I still remember the stinging pain. But it's a metaphor most people can relate to.

I add, "It doesn't matter if they never see a sonnet again, nor if later on, they can't tell a sonnet from a sea snake. What matters is that it's a wonderful English practice for training the mind to write, to think."

My colleague, fresh out of teacher college, replies, "Well, you go ahead and feed them that stuff. I'm working on dragon stories and relating it to video games. Call it gaming practice as English."

This brief hallway interchange compels me to think about my sonnet lessons, and that, in turn, brings me back to a little poetry project I've been working on for a few years. Finally, the conversation compels me to write the following essay:

Go Write Some Sonnets for the Things You Love

Go write some sonnets for the things you love, and you will feel their essence rise above the simple status of being described. The very structure, grace, and poignancy of words crafted into sonnet form cast such a different light onto any subject. That same light dances on the surface, exposes the subtleties, and illuminates the subject's core. But regarding the ideas of love and nature, the sonnet illuminates sublime.

I do not recall when it first occurred to me that *writing* sonnets might be just as interesting and challenging as *reading* them. For years, however, I have sipped the fine wine of the sonnet. Some vintages are palpably delicious, while others have a taste that baffles, intrigues, piques, and sometimes even perplexes. Naturally, then, sonnets have become the root of my love for poetry in general. Maybe that's why I decided to harvest the fruits of my study and begin to produce my own elixir of language. And so, one day I began *writing* sonnets.

My first attempts belonged not in the metaphorical wine cellar with Wordsworth, Donne, or Keats. No, my first sonnets were far from the fineness of Shakespeare in those classic catacombs. My first attempts belonged on the kitchen spice shelves—they were more like vinegar than fine wine. But with time, patience, practice, and a constant return to the roots for inspiration, I began to acquire a "taste" for words that worked.

So, let me offer you a glass of wine, and we'll leave the metaphor behind, and I'll share some of my sonnet experiences. Mind you, I'm still learning this craft. You might even be better at it than I if you start, or if you already are a sonneteer.

Rewind many years to Colorado University. I am a freshman, fresh out of Boulder High School college prep. I earned A's in English. I signed up for English 399 Milton, just to try on an upper division course for size. Nobody had truly defined *hubris* for me yet, and so I blithely attended an experienced scholarly gathering as a novice. I was inept at grasping the complexities of Milton and his important role in classic British literature. Intimidated by erudition, I remained silent much of the time, so they let me stay. On final exam day, I couldn't answer the essay prompts—not one of them. But I did learn a lot during the course, and I had iambic pentameter running through my bloodstream. So, I wrote a poem for my professor. It was a poem about growing up, signing up for the wrong class, and realizing just how much there was out there that I didn't know. I wrote for the entire two-hour final exam session. I wrote several hundred lines, all of it in heroic couplets. That's right, I wrote it entirely in paired lines of complete-thought Iambic pentameter. I must have included some of my new found Miltonian knowledge as well, for I received a B- in the course. I probably deserved a C. But I survived.

Much later in my academic journey, I took British Literature and *really* studied the versification of poetry and the artistic style of the sonnet. It was fun. I even began to memorize a few of my favorites. Sonnet 73 by Shakespeare was perhaps my first. But I still had not thought about penning a sonnet.

Then I finished college, landed a job as a backcountry guide in the summer and a ski patrolman in the winter, and I sort of forgot about sonnets. I didn't forget about poetry though. And as nature flooded my existence, I continued to put my impressions into poetry and song lyrics. I became a sort of musical voice for ski parties, a singing cowboy for the ranch, and a banjo playing boatman for the river. It was a good life, but there was no health insurance and not much security. My girlfriend, who later became my wife, reminded me about things like security and health insurance. And we both knew that earning a living by writing and singing poetry was, well, unlikely. So, I went back to school and got my teaching credential.

And that leads me back to the sonnet. Now I was on the other side. I was teaching sonnets to my English students rather than being taught them by my professors. Again, it was fun! When we broached the subject of iambic pentameter, I'd have a whole class bouncing their heads, tapping their desks, even waving their arms in metrical time. "That TIME of YEAR thou MAY'ST in ME be HOLD" would be recited in a sort of dancing, singsong silly fashion over and over again until they, my students, got the rhythm. We'd do this for Shakespeare's plays as well, but the sonnets were the most fun.

Alas, there were many other things to teach in English—vocabulary, grammar, stories, novels, essays et al. So, sonnet study was more of a short memorable moment. Then I took over the AP Literature class. *Versification* was back in the driver's seat. I thoroughly enjoyed relearning and then teaching the various forms of foot in meter. The Iamb was joined by the Trochee, Spondee, Anapest, and Dactyl. My students named the last one "terrible-dactyl" claiming that it should die like the dinosaur, so hard was it to master. Herrick's poem "Gather Ye Rose Buds" fit the bill superbly for the Dactyl because I could also refer to it when showing the film *Dead Poets Society*. Next, I could discuss the Anapest's application in Longfellow's "Paul Revere's Ride," mention that Clement Clarke Moore utilized this same meter in "T'was The Night Before Christmas," and then continue to tease the style with Dr. Seuss' anapestic adaptation in "The Grinch Who Stole Christmas."

But I always returned to the Iamb and was always looking for ways to teach it. Because of this, one day in a fit of creative frenzy, I assigned winter sonnets to the entire class.

"Write a sonnet about winter," I said. "It must use the proper rhyme scheme, and it must demonstrate a reasonable attempt at iambic pentameter." Everybody groaned. I spent the next two class periods coaching iambic meter like a swim coach teaches treading water. Then I got frustrated, stopped the class short, and said, "Ok, look, it's not that hard. Here, let's do one together!" We then wrote a sonnet on the old chalkboard as a class, or rather I wrote a sonnet while extracting ideas from students along the way. We first brainstormed ideas. Topic: simple things in nature. Here's how the sonnet panned out:

Simplicity Sonnet

Delight in moments wafting on warm winds
Like sun on shoulders or a bird's sweet tune,
Enticing us to pause, to peer within
To where the simple joyous pleasures bloom.
Discrepancies between desire and time
Will oft succumb to life's complexities,
And only will our intuitive mind
Halt the needless, stop frivolities.
Deciphering the most important dreams
Takes years of flustered hours badly passed
Through which we learn to finally perceive
What's worth the time when time's not long to last.
When nature's simple bliss is in the air,
The time to spend a thought is worth the care.

The neat thing was that half of my students actually turned out decent sonnets! Wow, sonneteers at age 17! I was impressed.

After that event, for me, there was no turning back. You see, it was so much fun crafting that sonnet with the English class that I kept on going. I've got twenty or so now in the file, but being somewhat of a transcendentalist in nature, my favorites are my recent attempts to produce acrostic sonnets for the equinoxes and solstices. My first acrostic sonnet was actually *close* to a solstice sonnet. But near Thanksgiving when we were learning sonnets, it was still a month away from the solstice. So, I wrote this one:

Winter's First, A Month Away

Onward through the fading light, we go,
Not sure we are prepared for days to come—
These winter nights oft frosted with white snow
Have made us wistful, longing for the sun.
And yet the season's cold has just commenced
Now to grasp us in its icy chills,
Keeping summer dreams so far distanced—
Safe locked beyond the leagues of whitened hills.
Gone are the leaves, the flowers, butterflies,
Instead, the slush and snow drifts cold and wet,
Voluminous the clouds occlude the skies
Icing the sun even more coldly yet.
Next month, however, the Winter Solstice means
Growing light, for six months, more sunbeams!

I didn't get to penning the acrostic seasonal sonnets until several years later, however. It took a particularly boring staff development day on the subject of integrating the new common core to cause me to doodle out phrases and realize that *winter solstice* itself has the perfect number of fourteen letters:

Winter's Nocturn

When angles of the sun are shining low,
Intuition tells us we must sleep.
Nocturnal tracks appear now in the snow
To mark the chilly vigil some must keep.
Enlightened constellations rule the skies,
Reminding us that distant worlds must be,
So vast the universe, so short our eyes.
Omniscience sets imagination free.
Light festivals will keep us from the dark,
So long the nights, so chilly and so cold.
The landscape seems now barren and now stark
In spite of seeds of summer that it holds.
Cold winter's night now turns the other way—
Envisions six months hence the longest day.

After writing the two winter sonnets, my thoughts naturally turned toward spring, and more ideas arose from an endeavor to playfully review the form of sonnet before AP test season. (I told students that it would be quite embarrassing to get a sonnet test question and not recognize the form of sonnet). So, this poem evolved for the vernal equinox, which by the way is thirteen letters long—one short of fourteen and problematic for creating another acrostic sonnet. After debating ideas such as "A Vernal Equinox" and "Vernal's Equinox" I settled on simply, "Spring is Coming." And for my AP students, test season was coming as well!

Springsong Sonnet

Sublime are changes deep within the ground,
Presenting tips of green through bulging earth,
Releasing buds with flowers all around,
Incensed air filling with rebirth.
Now reaching skyward buds adorn the trees,
Great rushing sap will rise within each arm
In time to burst alive with new green leaves
Suffused with light, such iridescent charm.
Come back all creatures who've been six months gone,
Or hibernated long within cocoons,
My garden anxiously awaits your song,
In melodies of green, I'll revel soon.
Now spring's first day has dawned its balanced sun,
Go breathe and sing and laugh and stretch and run.

Teaching without days off from spring break all the way into the first week of June often left me drained of creativity and badly in need of a recharge. My wife and I always spent the summer solstice out there somewhere, away from population and technology, and even away from my creative writing pursuits. One pre-solstice June day found me sitting in the airport awaiting a flight, notepad in hand, and that's when my summer solstice sonnet came to fruition. It also came with the ironic realization that *summer solstice* also has exactly fourteen letters to it—an idea that had evaded my attention while concentrating so hard on winter and spring. Summer's like that, it can creep up on you!

Summer full

So much effulgence greets the wandering eyes,
Unveiling life, which burgeons from the trees.
Meandering with the sounds and scents that rise
Midway between the breaths of morning's breeze.
Each moment seems to stretch the endless day,
Revolving to the ever-present sun,
So does the solstice subtly slip away
On golden stems where harvest's now begun.
Like magic floating on the fragrant air,
Sublimity of ease beneath warm skies
Takes all old struggles, all the wintry cares
Into green fields, to let them free and fly.
Come to the feast, it' time to celebrate
Each moment, from this dawn to dusk so late.

And so that brings me full circle to autumn, that time of year when teaching goes once again into full swing. I admit I'm still working on finding the perfect words for a decent autumn equinox sonnet. "Autumnways" using the fourteen-word phrase "Autumn Now Comes" is a start. Ok, so this one's not done yet. Maybe it will be easier to write next fall when the season's change is a bit more poignant. Maybe you can finish it?

Autumnways

And now the circle brings seasons around
Until the harvest nears its burgeoned fill.
The frost that greets the morns without a sound
Unleashes ice and snow of winter's chill . . .

M
N
N
O
W
C
O
M
E
S

I know that my iambic pentameter is a bit fuzzy at times. I also use some pretty simplistic, mostly masculine rhyme. Maybe you someday can improve upon these as well.

So, go and write a sonnet for something or someone you love! Why should Shakespeare have the corner on such a fun linguistic puzzle? Maybe we'll bring something back into the world of poetry where rhyme and meter seem to have faded like a sunset in autumn. If poetry can still be written by the pen, then style that's pure can surely rise again.

Sonnets are not starter songs, which is where this chapter began. Yet songs, especially folk songs, are replete with rhythm and rhyme. Lately, I find myself corralling all the wild dactyls, anapests, spondees, trochees, and the ever so domesticated iambs into the arena of starter songs. On a good year, students will argue whether or not a poem is more anapestic than dactylic, iambic or a-rhythmic. So now let's see what happens when we put Clement Clarke Moore, Henry Wadsworth Longfellow, and Theodor Giesel in the same room together.

Chapter 4: On The Rocks

A narrow ledge above the classroom whiteboard frame makes a perfect home for small, unobtrusive objects: a quality spare pen, my laser pointer procured from the pet store, a dollar's worth of change for an emergency run to the vending machines, an extra guitar pick, etc. Most of the items escape notice, which is the point of their placement. But on one end of the board ledge, I keep a subtly visible collection of ten to twelve pocket-sized stones, judiciously gathered from near the summits of local mountains I've hiked. I pick these eroded shards for their shapes, which match the profile of the peak; I also write the summit name on them with a marker. There they sit, innocuously inert yet charged with memories. Once in a while, however, someone notices them. The ensuing conversation goes something like this:

A student notices the rocks, and in particular one specific name. She exclaims, "Hey, I hiked Mount Timpanogas last summer with my family!"

"Wow Jessica, that's one of the best around. Did you do the eighteen-mile round trip loop?"

"Yeah, but Mom and my little brother stopped below the top. They were pooped. But my other brother John, my dad and I made it all the way up!"

"Did you see the mountain goats!"

"Oh, they were so *white*! And there were wildflowers everywhere."

"Yep, that's Timp for you. Ever hiked Bald Mountain over in the Uintas? It's really short but really beautiful. Sometimes it has goats too. I'll bet your mom and little brother could easily manage it."

"Uh, how do you get to it?"

"It's easy, just drive up the Mirror Lake Highway to the pass, go a hundred yards up the bumpy dirt road on the left that takes off right on top of the pass, and park there. It's only two miles up to the summit, and Bald Mountain is even higher than Timp."

"Neat. We go to the Uintas every summer. I'll take everybody up."

"Go early in the morning, though, because thunderstorms come up pretty quickly in that mountain range."

"Ok."

"Oh yeah, one more thing." I reach up to the ledge and grab a rock. It has Bald Mtn written on it in sharpie. Handing it to Jessica I say, "This one needs to go back."

Although rocks make their way into the writing topic plan during the year, I rarely hand these particular rocks to students and urge them to return them. But when a particularly observant student notices the rocks and our conversation outside of the planned curriculum indicates that they are avid hikers and have never been to where the rock came from, well it's simply a fun way to say, "You should go there!" When administrators talk about teachers needing to relate to their students, get to know them, get involved in their interests and passions—well, this seems to be a great example.

One unusual year I gave the entire collection to a group of uniquely curious graduating seniors, assigning each to return the stones home. Two of those graduates brought me rocks from places I have yet to go. I promised to return the rocks someday, except for perhaps the little stone brought to me from atop the Grand Teton. I'm not much of a technical climber. By the next school year, I had five more little rocks from five more local summits on the ledge (plus the two new ones) but nobody mentioned them. The year after I added four more. They weren't major mountains by any stretch, just wonderful hikes to high points near home, usually marked with a little altitude x and a name on the topographic maps. Most of them I've hiked multiple times—someday I'll look down and find a very familiar-looking rock.

Where the mountains touch the sky, much inspiration flows. One stormy day from deep in the jumbled up valley of public education challenges and dilemmas, without even realizing what I was doing, I shouted to those same mountains for help, for a creative solution to a pressing problem. One mountain, in particular, echoed an answer.

This story begins with an overstuffed folder in the back of my old four drawer metal file cabinet. Most of the items in it would make any educator cringe. They run the gamut from suicide notes to love letters, from blatant plagiarism examples to absurd administrative edicts. They represent those moments in public education that are stinking with psychology, liability, frustration, and total exasperation. I call it my "What Do I Do With This?" folder.

Several suicide threat stories, poems, and notes made their way into the file over the years. Each one was accompanied by a conference session with a counselor, and luckily for me, all got the attention they needed. Plagiarism examples and notes on how I dealt with each find their way into the file, along with the occasional exasperating responses from parents denying the act and defending their child despite hard, incontrovertible evidence. Several test cheating answer sheets that show letter for letter identical multiple-choice answers are there. Every answer is wrong.

That particular time I suspected the cheat and rearranged the questions before the test. The two offenders had indeed memorized the answers correctly—that is they memorized the old answers. In the days before electronic testing, rewriting a test seemed hard, but it was much easier than catching cheating through today's Snap Chat. I also included a simple end-of-year eight parts of speech summative assessment where a student who sat through two trimesters of English with a daily routine of studying the parts of speech scored one point out of twenty-five. When I asked him what was going through his mind he said, "Waterskiing and girls." Several very profane short stories and essays made it into the file, as did the notes on the anatomy lesson I gave the writers, explaining that there are ways of being profane without violating school rules regarding expletives. There's a few "English sucks" notes in there, some bribe offers, several hate and racism letters directed at many targets (fortunately not me), some of which I had to report to the authorities. Sometimes I receive direct writings about sexual abuse. Again, those get reported and I treat those students with extra patience and compassion, but I don't open up any conversations regarding those—that's a bit beyond my training. The file holds numerous bullying letters (and my replies to them discussing karma and insecurities), and many examples of the worst student work I've ever seen. I saved substitute reports that didn't follow one inch of my lesson plans (not asked to come back) and substitute reports that explained a sort of *Lord of the Flies* type classroom day (also not asked to return). The file does hold one sub report that was clear, professional, but also a scathingly honest report on one certain students' behavior. I sent a photocopy to mom. There's an envelope with four squares of blotter acid in there (hmm, maybe I should dump that one), and every kind of drug culture writing you can imagine. A community apology letter made it in there explaining that when the local newspaper printed the journalism class story about the cheerleaders' pom dance, the "word processor" separated the *m* for column spacing, thus making it a "porn dance." The list goes on. Fully half of the folder is made up of professional dilemmas as well: administrative faux pas, colleague indiscretions, district inanities and more—enough to generate an entire book on the trials and tribulations in the trenches of public education.

I'll admit that much of this folder contains challenging and difficult scenarios and is often quite negative. Once in a while, however, a bit of special history slides into the file almost unnoticed. The other day my hand got stuck in this folder while searching for a lesson plan. I was trying to cram the contents further back to release my hand, but when I pulled my fingers out, an old photocopied map stuck up and wouldn't go back down neatly. Almost irritated, I jammed the thick file against the back of the cabinet and crammed the map back into its place—*almost.*

Almost is the key word here. I paused, pulled the now somewhat wrinkled map back out, and it seemed to say, *Remember me? I'm a difficulty transformed into a positive.*

"Ah," I said out loud, "You *are* a good memory!"

The map represented a teaching moment that almost became an overly negative event. Instead, the moment went from seriousness to serendipity, from frustration to fascination, and from crudity to curiosity.

It's year seven as English teacher in picturesque rural mountain Utah, and I'm returning from lunch to my roomy, high ceilinged classroom with a stack of photocopies. Most of the kids are still in the cafeteria, but several groups are lounging on the nice stone benches in the wide, mall-style halls, waiting for the bell. This includes a bunch of misfits who hang together. As I approach the somewhat anachronistic group, I see two boys in low-rider jeans facing away from me talking to another who is sporting a stylistically torn sweatshirt. The fourth is a numbskull from my basic-level Junior English class.

Sweatshirt sees me coming, makes an elbow lift, finger down cool pose gesture and says to me, "Four Twenty Dude!"

Lowrider turns and smirks, "Yeah, Four Twenty!"

I shake my head, about to get mad, when Numbskull comments, "Doherty, you *had* to do drugs, didn't you?"

But I'm ready. It's not the first time that question has been posed. And it's about the twentieth time this month someone has blurted out "Four Twenty" to me and other faculty members. To the question, my pat reply, "Sorry guys, I was too busy during high school and college for drugs." It's at least a partially honest reply. It actually wasn't until college that I dabbled, but I would *never* let on *anything of the sort* to my students. I figure that honesty and rights are evolving issues at the high school level—best left to professional interpretation. To the irritatingly recurring "four twenty" blurt, I continue my current strategy.

"Ok, guys. It took me a while to figure out what you meant by shouting four-twenty. Now it's just getting old. You can't even tell me what it means."

"Sure we can," sneers Lowrider, "It means do drugs, man. It means smoke pot. Do it at four-twenty."

Not wanting to reopen the debate I'd engaged in with several students earlier, I smile wanly, shake my head and walk away. They laugh, and again I hear, "Four Twenty, Doherty." Of course, it's not "Mister Doherty," it's just the standard disrespectful last name rendition. Irritation number one now added to irritation number two. The concept of pot, leaves drawn on notebooks, blackboards, or bathroom walls never bothered me beyond the graffiti factor. After all, I grew up in Boulder, Colorado during the late Sixties. Pot, LSD, and a whole lot of other drugs were plentiful as fruit on the trees but teaching in a zero-tolerance school regarding drug culture always forced me to censor whatever I saw whenever found it.

During the short walk back to my room, I remember irritation number three and dial my office phone for a quick call before the fifth-hour bell.

"Gary? Mark here. Say, we need to block another internet site. Yeah, it's coming up simply as 'Four-Twenty,' either the numbers or spelled out. You get a great big pot leaf right off on the screen. Yeah, it's that counterculture drug site stuff kids keep spouting in the halls. Might want to mention it to Mrs. Bushell in case she has a chance to watch some of the kids in the library."

"Ok, good. I'll tell Alene, but she doesn't catch much on the computers. She'd have to stand right behind them all the time, and they're not close enough to her desk."

"Well, I'm personally glad she cares more about books than computers, but I guess technology is here to stay."

Gary chuckles, "I sure hope so, otherwise, I'll be out of a job. Thanks, Mark, Bye."

As I hang up the phone, I think to myself, Well, *at least it's Friday, good May weather. Might be time to get away from this school crap, head to the Uintas, maybe Hayden Peak or Bald Mountain. People will start hiking them soon and I want to be sure the summit registers still have pages to sign.*

I was planning on "recharging" before the next week of teaching. My wife and I loved to hike up mountains, and we had been maintaining summit registers (notebooks and pencils stuffed in old green army surplus ammo cans) on top of two popular peaks so that hikers could sign their names when they conquered the mountain—an old but endearing tradition.

We were residing at that time, during the mid-1990s, in a tiny 450 square foot cabin in Samak at the edge of the Uinta Mountains. We were in the process of recycling the place into a starter home for year-round living. My school, South Summit High, was a beautiful, new, steep blue roofed dark red brick building located at the edge of town on the Mirror Lake Highway. Its 450 students were a mixture of old farming families and new bedroom community families. Salt Lake City was only 40 miles away. In short, we had a nice mix of kids, ranging from rodeo cowboys to lawyers' and doctors' progeny. We had the gifted, the garrulous, and the groupies. But the best part was that as teachers, our classes rarely exceeded twenty-five students. As I look back now, I clearly see the difference in education and intimate learning from where I stand now in the trenches of urban Salt Lake City with nearly 40 kids in every class. That intimacy (which I left to help my wife pursue her career) is perhaps what makes the rest of this memory so compelling, so unique.

The lovely weekend of hiking ends, Monday comes quickly enough. Even at the rural school level, work is still work. By third hour the first "Four Twenty" is blurted out dead center during silent reading time. I am finishing the writing lesson on the chalkboard and momentarily flush, then without even turning around I speak in loud, authoritative, teachery tones, "Twelve, Four, Seventy-Nine."

Silence.

"Twelve Four, Seventy-Nine," I say again, turning around and looking straight at Numbskull who has interrupted reading.

"What's that mean?" Numbskull retorts.

I repeat, "Twelve, Four, Seventy-Nine. You figure it out . . . *Four Twenty*. And by the way, thanks for wrecking reading time. Ok, seven minutes more, and a free test question hint for everyone if it stays quiet for the *whole* seven minutes."

Numbskull opens his book, pretends to read, but makes a melodramatic, question-y wrinkly face in the direction of one of his buddies two rows away. They are seated apart from each other for practical reasons. His buddy mouths the number I just spouted. And at that moment, I realize that I've got them, got them all, every four-twenty kid in the school.

After class Numbskull and Buddy come up to me. "So what's twelve four seventy-nine mean?"

I reply, "It means a lot more than Hitler's birthday or some random time of day. Maybe it has something to do with the chemical composition of THC. You guys figure it out."

Meanwhile, during writing lesson time, I had scrawled out the numbers twelve four seventy-nine on the chalkboard, just in case someone forgot and mixed up a digit. As Numbskull and Buddy walk out of the room, I look up at the lovely high ceiling with soaring thoughts. I'm thinking, *It's so simple! It sounds like a date but could be a figure. It rolls off the tongue. I can run with this, and it will take them plenty of time to catch me. This time I'm in control of the amusement park ride!*

For days, every time I heard Four Twenty, I replied, "Twelve four seventy-nine." Whenever I saw Lowrider, Numbskull, Sweatshirt and even a few of Slouchpant's groupies, I called out the number without even waiting to hear Four Twenty. And like mosquitoes smelling blood, they pestered me about it.

"Is it a date? Is it the date they invented marijuana?" asked Numbskull one day in front of the whole class.

"Maybe you'd better do a little research. And no, I think they *invented* marijuana a little earlier than that. But I'll give you a hint, it *does* relate to drug culture, at least indirectly."

Within a day, even the classy students were curious and asking questions. One of my juniors, Shaun Phillips, came in after school with his girlfriend Marci Brown.

He started grilling me. "Is it a penal code? How about a math problem? Is it science, or is it history? C'mon, give us a few hints!"

I relented. "Ok. I'll give out one hint each day until someone figures it out. Whoever figures it out will get a prize."

"What's the hint?" asked Marci eagerly.

"Not so fast. I'll post the hint on my door tomorrow morning."

"Aw, now we have to wait," moaned Shawn. "It's only lunchtime."

I thought to myself, *Whew, lunchtime, that gives me a few hours to concoct some good hints, and I guess I'd better think up a prize too.*

Then I grabbed an extra sheet of white paper and scrawled in sharpie, *12 4 79 Hint One: It has to do with our state.*

And thus, began the hinting phase. The hints went something like this: *It is related to maps. It is related to physiology and health also. Certain athletes seek it out. It is free but requires experience. There is a t-shirt designed that states its theme. The legal drugs, endorphins, are involved. It is a geographical place.* The last hint was enough. And it was sandy-haired Shawn, undoubtedly with the help of his smart, freckle-faced girlfriend Marci, who finally guessed it.

"We've got it!" someone called out as six or seven kids paraded into my room shortly after the 3:30 bell. "We've found your Twelve Four Seventy-Nine! It's here, on the map, Hayden Peak!"

Indeed, the numbers 12 4 79 serendipitously popping into my head earlier represented 12,479 feet, the elevation of Hayden Peak. It was one of the mountains our summit registers rested upon.

Shawn was at the lead, holding the map, but another kid was talking anxiously for him.

"Ok, ok, nice job everybody!" I smiled, turning from my chalkboard and dusting my hands off. "Now, exactly *who* was the one who discovered it?"

They all looked at Shawn, some making gestures. "He did, but we helped!!"

"All right. So how many other people did you tell just now."

Shane replied, "Uh, I think nobody."

"Good. I've got a prize for all six, uh, seven of you, but you've got to keep it a secret until lunch tomorrow. I'll award prizes during lunch here in my room."

"James helped him too," added Marci, the only girl in the group. "He found the map."

"Does James know the final answer yet?"

"Uh, no, he's not here today."

"Fine, James gets an award too. So tomorrow— I'll ask Principal Moser if I can make an addition to the morning announcements. Sound good?"

They all nodded.

"Remember, it's a secret still until lunch."

The next morning, I stopped by the faculty copy machine and made a blowup section of a specific topographic map quadrangle featuring Hayden Peak. Then I began carefully dotting the route and lettering sections, "big boulders," "scramble to saddle," "snow gully in spring," "stay left of big block rock," "narrow rock ridge, hands and knees" and so forth.

By lunchtime the next day I was equipped with photocopies of my hand-altered map, eight jumbo sized chocolate bars, and the hiking guide. Fifty kids streamed into my room at the lunch bell. Just before placing a transparency of the map on the overhead projector, my speech went something like this:

"The Twelve Four Seventy Nine mystery has been solved! Before I award the tenacious winners, let me say that this response to Four Twenty is also related to drugs, except that they are the legal ones: endorphins and adrenaline. It's also related to the t-shirt that reads, *Get High, Go Climb a Mountain.* Honorable mentions and helper awards, these jumbo chocolate bars, are just the kind of treat that will taste wonderful if you actually make it all the way up there."

Calling out each name, I delivered the chocolate with a folded map attached to each bar.

"And now, Shawn Phillips, I award you the Twelve Four Seventy Nine prize, your own jumbo chocolate bar, and a brand new copy of *Hiking and Climbing in the Uinta Mountains.*"

As I said this, I turned on the overhead projector with the map showing Hayden Peak, 12,479' in elevation. Everyone cheered and clapped as I handed Shawn his prize. Numbskull, Lowrider, and Sweatshirt were also present, seeming to enjoy the proceedings, seeming to have forgotten Four Twenty for at least the moment. It was indeed the end of the brief reign of Four Twenty at South Summit High.

On my two-mile bicycle commute home, a tickly little thought occurred to me. *What if one of those kids actually goes up there with my hand-marked map, falls off the mountain and gets hurt?* Fortunately, that never happened, but the uncomfortable tickle of possibility gave me pause on several occasions. I sensed I needed always to urge caution, training, and even finding guides for those students who seemed likely to get involved in mountaineering.

And the somewhat misplaced map in the *What Do I Do With This* file? It's still hiding out in there. It remains there as a reminder that there's more than one way of dealing with a Numbskull.

Chapter 5: Cairns and Summit Registers

Mountains are big. Their great shadows reach my classroom from afar. Their stories and their settings are as poignant as the sea. Headwater, streams, falls, cascades, cool clear lakes, crags rocks and cliffs, forests of trees, wilderness and wild animals, flowers and snow—ecology and geology—most good things come from the mountains. And so do challenges: blizzards, avalanches, rockfalls, fires, lighting rain and hail, bitter cold with icy winds, wild animals and insects, exhaustion, hypothermia, and death. For humans, mountains have always been there to cross, climb, conquer, love, cherish, and dream about—even pray from. And yes, mountains have always been obstacles—dangerous, fearsome, loathsome, evil, impossible, and even mythological.

In the realm of teaching, there are as many texts written about mountains as there are large rocks in a mile of river. I thought I'd pondered and mulled over every type of mountain-related text in my quest to teach great writing that was readable for students. Then one day I found a new text. Like a sneaky fox, it evaded my searching eyes, yet all the while it was living right beneath my nose.

Perhaps the reason my wife Deborah and I bought the tiny cabin in Rural Utah with no water or plumbing to slowly remodel it into a small, year-round, livable home was due to our discovery of one of the greatest easy mountain climbs in the state. It's a short two-mile hike from the pass and it surveys the entire High Uinta Wilderness, but better yet, it's only accessible by foot. Granted, there are numerous places in the Uintas that are only accessible by foot, but none so spectacular, none so close to the road, none so special. This spot is Bald Mountain, elevation 11,943 feet (3,640 meters). On our first visit to the Uintas, we hiked the trail two miles up to the summit. Nobody was there. Upon returning, we observed a cabin for sale. It was near enough to Park City and Salt Lake City for commuting, but far enough out to feel really rural. We bought the cabin and moved in. I applied for a teaching job at the high school two-miles from the small town of Kamas and landed a position. The small town of Kamas was uniquely both rural and suburban. Dotted with ranches and farms, the valley took us back a hundred years in time, yet many of the residents worked as professionals in Salt Lake City, forty miles away.

While living for eight years, near Kamas, we trained for other outdoor hiking and climbing trips on other mountains using the Bald Mountain Trail as our workout, visiting it as much as once a week, learning its moods, loving its quiet times. During the months of August and September, we frequently made after-school sunset treks, hiking through the slanting light of waning summer evenings. Those alpenglow evenings astride the Uinta Mountains linger vividly in my memory.

Not long after first hiking the trail, we noticed that the old mailbox summit register on top had been smashed flat. Soon thereafter, someone chucked it over the edge. And what an edge it is, dropping nearly 2,000 feet straight down to Mirror Lake. The east face is one of those look-down-between-your-toes-into-the-abyss precipices.

Furthermore, no one had taken care of the register for many years, as evidenced by a jumble of papers stuffed in the box dating back nearly ten years to the late 1980's. So, we decided to purchase a surplus 30 caliber ammo can and start a new register for the busy months of July, August, and September when Bald Mountain Trail is melted off and the hike is accessible to anyone with the heart and the lungs for getting an endorphin and altitude high.

A couple of times the box disappeared (someone just *had* to have that $3.95 ammo can), but the notebooks were usually left somewhere, tucked somewhere into the boulders near the summit cairn. Once the can was left open and soaked by storm, but the notebooks dried out later and they were still readable. And so, for a glorious period of seven years, the Bald Mountain Summit Register again thrived. And we thrived on our training missions to restock it with notebooks and see what wonderful writings were left behind.

The register. What about the register? What a wonderful thing, a summit register. What a wonderful tradition. Over the period of those eight years some remarkable entries made it into those notebooks. And those notebooks made it into my files at school. Then one day I realized what a great teaching tool those entries would make. By the next day, my students were reading the entries with me. A sort of naturally inspired wordsmithing marked many the register's entries—lines shone like emeralds. For many people, Bald Mountain was their *first* mountain. For others, it was one of their most inspirational mountains. Due to the fact that Bald Mountain's summit is only two miles from the highway, it is attainable during the summer for most healthy people with a willing spirit. It is a moderate, rocky hike with a lot of steps-up, but no scrambling or climbing needed. And so many people who would never consider truly climbing a mountain, but like hiking and adventure, find themselves on top of a truly spectacular mountain. They *feel* like they have climbed a huge mountain. Their spirits soar. Their poetry becomes sublime, their humor inspired. And then they notice the summit register. One year, along with the requisite Bald Mtn. 11,943' on the cover, I penned in sharpie "I came, I saw, I signed." Here are a few samples from these inspired hikers:

9-1-98 Take a moment, breathe deeply and take in the world. From here there are no real problems, only life and living. Ed Edwards Florida (the flatlands)

9-1-98 Thanks to Ed of the flatlands. Live the moment. . . all of time is compressed in the "now" of this moment. Colleen

9-4-98 There are no words to express the magnificence. Standing on top of the world, my husband and kids with me experiencing the freedom of soaring. If I were an eagle, I would soar. What an awesome feeling of power and freedom, Life is perfect.

Jennifer, Jim, Bradon (age 6 years), and Kolten (age 2 ½) Jorgason. Sandy, Utah

8-19-98 We had to wait until evening to do this because of weather. It was worth it. I last did this 40 years ago. It's still wonderful, but now I'm doing it with my daughter instead of my parents. I hope she gets to do it with her kids. Curt Tulison

8-18-2001 I believe that friends are quiet angels that lift us to our feet when our wings have trouble remembering how to fly . . I can't believe it! I finally made it! Devin Burr

9-23-2001 Today we soared with the eagle and touched the sky. There is no war or hatred or fear here, only God's gift of beauty. Laurie & Reed

10-7-01 This hike was awesome, the view spectacular. I have hiked many mountains in my life since I was 12 yrs. old. I'm glad that I get to add this to my list. Climbing mountains is like our life, it can be hard, windy, & cold or the sun beating down nonstop causing sunburns, but the challenge and getting to the top is a feeling that only by experiencing it can you truly understand. Laurie C

9-7-98 The beauty of places like this comes not from man & his accomplishments but from the realization of how small and insignificant we really are compared to the marvelous expanse of God's creation. Amazing! Vileena B. Begay 20

6-28-02 The world is a beautiful expression of God and is to be preserved forever. Vincent T. Nguyen

10-21-01 Took three days to get here, but it was worth every step. Storms a' comin' in. We had to kill a mountain goat because we ran out of food. Great hiking! Marylynn Butler

10-21-01 Hi Mom. Holy cow there are a lot of rocks! Beauty View! Aaron Watson

7-31-03 Well, none of us died and we made it finally!! Halston Magg

7-24-03 AAAAAaaaaaaah . . .. SPLAT

7-2-03 Great view, lots of goats. Snow not too bad. Wish I knew more about my new camera. Glad I can hike to such great places. Mike

7-26-03 This sight is the way life was meant to be seen. Live and let live, love and let love, be and let be. Open eyes and awake from your delusions, awake from your dream, and transcend with me. Vira Petranovich

11-3-03 We had five people and the oldest one made it first! He is 71 years old and whipped all of us! That truly is an awesome sight. I'm glad my grandpa could make it up here with me. Thanks Gramps! David

Every autumn at school, about the time when the first snows closed the high trails and passes, I would bring out a new set of notebooks from Bald Mountain's summit register box. My students and I read them, wondered at them, exclaimed about them, and wrote poems, stories, and essays inspired by the entries. It amazed me that out of the dozens of notebooks retrieved from the register on Bald Mountain, I found less than ten pages of inappropriate language or content that I had to remove before letting high schoolers read them. Maybe I should have left the very few F-words, drug use mentions, and homophobic and religious slurs in the registers, but at that time I was trying to be conscious of the morality I presented in the classroom and I wanted them to see mountain hiking as nothing but good, clean, healthy fun as far away from the problems of culture and cities as one could get. People just aren't as twisted, I guess, when they go climb a mountain. Or maybe demented people don't climb mountains. Either way, it was an interesting observation. During the years we kept the register, people from nearly every state signed it, and people from at least twenty foreign countries penned their lines in their native languages. Students loved trying to translate the messages, as this was several years BG (Before Google).

I kept replacing the summit register notebooks until I moved from Kamas, the town dubbed "Gateway to the Uintas." When I left, I chose a cohort I deemed most likely to keep the tradition going due to his two stout, outdoorsy sons who dreamed of living and working near home. I still haul around some photocopies of the choicer entries from those logs, and every time I peruse them, I return instantly to the summit of my beloved Bald Mountain in Utah's Uinta Mountains, a stone's throw from a highway, from cars, trucks, ATVs, buses—but an eternity away from civilization.

Chapter 6: Venues, Classrooms, and Sheep

The first eleven years of my teaching career I taught in rural schools. What I knew for certain at the time was that rural areas were closer to the natural and wilderness areas that I absolutely could not live long without. The outdoors was the intoxicant upon which I would forever be hooked. What I learned, later on, was that the class sizes in rural schools were usually a third or a half as large as class sizes in an urban setting. When I moved into teaching in large urban schools, I lost a huge part of the magic of teaching—I lost the time for extended creative inspirations that I could craft into lessons. But I didn't lose the technique, nor the passion for bringing the outdoors into the classroom, and many of my lesson plans were already conceived and designed. What did happen was that the barren waste of city streets separating me from my beloved rocks, rivers, trees, and sky drove me more fiercely to incorporate nature and beauty and animals and wild things into my students' world and into my workspace called a classroom. Whenever people would approach me about my former work experiences, I would simply tell them that when I left rural school teaching, I left heaven on assignment to see if I could make a difference in the trenches. And then I'd smile, get a far-away look in my eye, and tell another story, like this one:

It is the last week of school in rural Kamas, a mere ten miles from the 2002 Utah Olympic Venue sites of Deer Valley and Park City. The resorts can be seen out my classroom windows in the distance. But outside these windows, another century suddenly steals the attention of my twenty-two Junior English students. When class starts, I own the undivided attention of my students. This is my year-end Edward Abbey essay readings of "Rocks" and "Water" from *Desert Solitaire.* The text is an attention-getter indeed, that is until a herd of 150 sheep stroll by the large plate glass floor to door lintel window in the corner of the classroom. The lesson, essays and all, grind to a sudden halt. Closure for the term and connections to our previously read authors Aldo Leopold, Rachel Carson, and Edward O. Wilson, will have to wait until the sheep pass.

Sheep do not normally graze on or near the school lawns. It is indeed a spectacle. Amidst chuckles and snorts from students, one junior blurts out, "It's just the Seeeeeeeniors practicing for graaaaduation." Everybody laughs. Another student, one literally obsessed with llamas, exclaims, "This herd should have a head llama to keep the coyotes away! Do you see the head llama?" Everybody rolls their eyes.

I shake my head, chuckling, then ask a student near my desk to phone the office and let them know that there is a herd of sheep loose in front of the school. Melanie, our secretary, scarcely does a double take and calls the local rancher who is undoubtedly missing his sheep, then she continues the year end wrap up work at her desk. Business as usual in Kamas. What? Don't sheep come grazing on the tasty green grass lawns of every American school?

Back in class and back on track, I refrain from making a number of readily available yet non-school appropriate sheep and Utah jokes. We continue with Edward Abbey. I am thinking about the fact that as little as ten years ago, Edward Abbey might be considered too risky to teach in an English class out West. But now, with the exception of a few essays containing profanities, Abbey's once radical views seem milk-toast compared to any given night on the television set. No wonder kids are having trouble discerning the meaning of boundaries.

The following day the sheep are, of course, long gone, but Melanie just happens to show up at my door asking to talk to one of my students—the same boy who made the jab about the seniors being sheep during the stampede.

"Can I see Jake for a moment," she asks as I pause from reading the last pages of the Abbey essay. Jake got called to the office often, usually for unpaid cafeteria lunches or library fines.

"As long as he's not done anything Baaaaaaaad," I reply. Laughter erupts, and a bit of mindless humor makes the perfect teaching moment to provide some balance to the cynical, intellectual humor of Edward Abbey.

Maybe in twenty years, those students will remember the lessons of Aldo Leopold, Rachel Carson, Al Gore, Edward O. Wilson, and good old Ed Abbey. Maybe they'll remember and appreciate a place and a time in which sheep could visit school and cause a stir and rouse humor amidst the rigors of education in the fast-paced modern world. Maybe they will vote, someday, to preserve open space, farm animals, and some of America's rural lifestyle. Sometimes the simplest events seem to have the greatest impacts. Memory and humor often walk hand-in-hand. I still remember the day; I wonder if any of my students do as well.

Immediately following the sheep show, I assigned one of my journalism students to write the story for the school news. The story fell a bit flat, so we never ran it, but it gave me an idea for a journalism lesson. After reading the flat sheep story to the class, including due apologies to the author, I gave students a practice story to write. I wrote up a set of imagined notes and asked them to write me three short pieces, one straight news, one feature story, and one editorial. The set of story notes went as follows:

- Escaped from trailer Friday
- South hallways doors propped open for large UPS delivery
- Stopped by school on way to state fair (FFA members)
- Chaos between first and second hours passing period
- Cornered next to office and finally recaptured
- Herded into entryway between doors so FFA officers could rope it when someone opened the inside door
- Weighing 300 lbs.
- Pig's name "Francis" was really frightened (named after nearby town)
- Nobody injured, including pig, despite lots of squealing
- "We've had some rodeos, but this was the wildest" Jim Appleton, FFA advisor & teacher
- "It could have caused serious injury" Alec Manwill, Principal
- "I'm sincerely sorry about the whole thing." Sam Sneed, FFA president
- "Evidently Sam forgot to latch the trailer properly. He'll never do that again" Jim Appleton

While students drafted their news stories, I decided to put together the creative writing story of the same imagined, yet ever so possible, rural school incident. Students turned out some wonderful stories, and a sense of humor prevailed, but more importantly, it gave me the perfect platform for demonstrating the difference between news, feature and editorial writing. And yes, there is a difference between journalism and creative writing, or at least there was back then! Here is my version of the short creative story:

Francis's Frolick

Alec Manwill, principal of South Summit High School, had great ears. Someone once said he could hear a senior sneaking out of the south doors and would be able to tell you what shoe type was doing the walking without ever leaving his office. So, it's no wonder that when he heard the tremendous trampling of feet coming down the long main corridor of the school, he was poised to snip out of his office, ready to grab, just as the noisy, trotting offenders reached him.

He assumed, of course, from the sound he heard that there were two students, probably boys, running fast down the hall. He assumed, he posed, and he launched out of his office at just the right moment, right into the face of Francis, the FFA Club's prize 300 lb. pig.

It's hard to say who was more surprised, Mr. Manwill or the pig. It's not hard to say who squealed the loudest. Francis screeched to a halt, slithering on the tile floor, turned and began scrabbling back down the hallway towards a veritable army of worried FFA students and friends zeroing in on their precious escaped prize pig.

After recovering from his shock and letting out a yelp which drew students out of the doors of several main hallway classrooms, Mr. Manwill took one step forward and fell flat on his back. He had slipped, you see, on something rather unpleasant left behind by a freaked-out pig with an upset stomach.

Meanwhile, Sam Sneed, the FFA president who had failed to properly latch the trailer Francis escaped from, started hollering to all the students who were now rubbernecking in the halls. "Stop that Pig!" he ordered, "Before she gets hurt!"

Halfway down her return run of the south hallway, Francis stopped, looking straight ahead at a crew of FFA officers, Sam in front, that stood between her and the opened doors of the south hallway. Then she turned around and saw the hallway behind her filling with curious onlookers. Principal Manwill was closing fast down the hallway.

With one last loud squeal, Francis turned again to the south and ran right through the FFA crew, out the South door, and right up into the trailer. It seems someone had hastily backed the trailer up against the doors, right next to the UPS guy who was waiting impatiently with a dolly full of packages, not daring to enter the melee.

"It was the easiest she's ever gone into the trailer," said Sam with a cheesy grin after the trailer door had been safely latched.

Principal Manwill wasn't too amused, and he stated that he would be scheduling a meeting with FFA members and their advisor. The bell for second hour rang, and everything got back to normal.

Whether it be the fact of the sheep or the fiction of the pig, the truth is that rural teaching fostered a creative atmosphere. First and foremost, in making this possible was the small class sizes and intimacy of rural schools; secondarily was the rural atmosphere and the proximity to the mountains and wilderness areas.

When teachers die and go to teaching heaven, I'm thinking they get a job in some wonderful rural area where there are as many animals as there are people, where classes are small, and horizons are huge.

Chapter 7: Arrowheads

Each time I bring the chunk of ripple rock out to use as a writing topic, reactions are similar. The fossilized waves are set about two inches apart, and the tops of the ripples are white, while the valleys and the rest of the sandstone piece is a maroonish red color. The rock is about eight by eight inches flat and an inch thick. I distinctly remember finding it lying on a slope of eroding Moenkopi sandstone on BLM land in the desert outside of Moab near the Colorado River. I always lift the rock high and display it to the class like an athlete presents a trophy and say, "How about *this* for the week's writing topic?"

"It looks like a slab of ribs," comments Jeremy. I detect a hint of derision in his voice. "Can I eat it?"

I hold the ripple rock flat, at eye level, waving my other hand over the top. "Now what do you think?"

"Oh, I get it," chimes Suzy. "It's waves in the sand!"

Jeremy snorts, "It's just a damn rock."

"Language, Jeremy," I reply firmly. "But no, it's not just a *damn* rock, nor is it a rock from a *dam*. It's also not an *inane* or *meager* or *incorporeal* or even a *vacuous* rock. Suzy is right. It's fossilized ripples in mud, from the Jurassic Era. It's the same mud dinosaurs used to step and leave tracks in."

"Uh," huffs Jeremy. "So how did it get made?"

"Ah," I reply, "That's for day two of writing, you know, the science-y stuff." I turn my attention to the class as a whole. "Today, let's talk about rocks as a metaphor in our language. But first, be sure to copy down Edward Abbey's quote from the board."

Then I recite Abbey's words orally, "*Lying within the bounds of a national monument, these rocks and artifacts are protected by law.*"

"Did you steal that rock from the national park?" asks Michael pointedly.

"No," I explain, "this one came from Bureau of Land Management (BLM) land. You know, land where grazing permits are allotted, oil is drilled for, mining happens. This rock was legally collected for the purposes of education. But I can tell you where I've found arrowheads and pot shards and fossils and other artifacts on lands protected by The Antiquities Act and left them right where I found them." I look hard at Michael, who seems to be appeased for the moment.

"We'll get to artifacts later, but right now let's brainstorm how something so elementary as a rock has become a metaphor in our language. Be sure to write down the brainstorm as we go." I then begin a quick dialogue with the class.

"If you can't swim, you do what?"

"Sink like a stone!"

"Metaphor one, state as a simple simile, write it down. A drinker who hasn't had a drink for days is not only said to be sober, but what kind of sober?"

"Stone cold sober!"

"Right. What's another name for a rough experience you have to endure?"

No answers.

"It's also the name of an ice cream."

"Rocky road!"

"Really old things or people are called old as a,"

"Fossil!"

"Yep, or you can call it stone age. Try this one, pot smokers get,

"Stoned!"

"Why in the heck do we equate being high with stones? I'll let you think about that one. Next, people who just won't change are called,"

"Stubborn as a rock!"

"Someone who you can count on, is really strong, always there for you is called,"

"BFF?"

"Try like a rock, or rock solid. Here's an easier one. They say when something is really close, it's just a,"

"Stone's throw away!"

"And what do they say about a rolling stone?"

"It's a rock musician?"

"Ha, good try. Haven't you heard the saying, *a rolling stone gathers no moss*? Ok, I guess it's a bit old. How about this one, If you get in trouble for telling the truth, but you also get in trouble for lying you're,"

"Between a rock and a hard place!"

"When they get it in writing, they might also say that it's,"

No answer.

"Set in stone. Haven't you heard that one before? Ok, one more. When things get so bad that you think they can't get any worse, you are said to have,"

"Hit rock bottom!"

"Ok, write me a page about rocks being used as a metaphor in our language. Why do you think this occurs? Weave all of the examples into your paragraph. Ten minutes, timer is on. Go.

As students begin to write, I glance at the poster-sized arrowhead chalk drawing hanging on the door and begin to reminisce. The drawing, a jar of colorful chert flakes (which are chippings left over from the process of arrowhead making), and the hunk of fossilized ripple rock all made their way early on into my boxes of writing topics. The chalk drawing eventually got unrolled, laminated, and hung sideways on the classroom door, pointing into the room with the words "Wilderness Boundary." The chert flakes landed in a plastic container for pass-around-the-class items, reserved for our unit on First People cultures, and the roughly six by six-inch chunk of ripple rock immediately became a key thought-provoking writing subject. All three items get revisited at the end of each year when we read Edward Abbey's essay "Rocks" from *Desert Solitaire* and make connections to fossils, arrowheads, and chert flakes. But for me, the arrowhead drawing holds the most significance. Here is why.

The first trade I made with Robert Fulghum back in 1989 was a cassette tape of my original music for a copy of his first book, *All I Really Need to Know I Learned in Kindergarten.* One of the last trades we made wasn't really a trade as much as it was an exchange of gestures. During his time in Southern Utah, I got to know Fulghum and his wife Lynn quite well, got to work on a crew building his house, got to witness his rise to fame. He got to witness a struggling musician trying to make ends meet, reluctant to grow up and take on a more responsible life. It was about that time when I met my wife Deborah, started seriously considering marriage for the first time at age thirty, and decided that maybe I should return to school to get a teaching credential. And that's where a special arrowhead came into play. I found the arrowhead on an old mining road in the LaSal Mountains near Pack Creek Ranch during the summer before I returned to school. It was only my second ever perfect point find. The two-inch-long arrowhead was finely flaked in red chert with precise symmetrical detail running from tip to dual notched tail. I carried it everywhere I went like a talisman in my pocket. I felt it most poignantly when working at the ranch, so near to where the lovely point seemed to have called out to me to notice and find it. And so, one night at the ranch, while playing guitar and singing for tips in order to pay the next term's tuition at school, Fulghum dropped in for dinner and we visited.

"I hear you've been staying in a fancy hotel in Grand Junction while taking classes." He smiled knowingly.

"Yeah, it's a-Ford-able. Ha, ha. And it's right on campus at Mesa State. I call it the camper shell room at the parking lot plaza."

"How many nights?"

"Just two, doing a Tuesday-Thursday schedule, so I drive over at five in the morning on Tuesday, then come home late Thursday. I've already gotten to know campus security, and they are ok with it. I stay in the library until it closes at midnight, then go catch a few hours of sleep until food service opens at six a.m. Told them I'd call if I saw any weird parking lot stuff anytime."

"Probably more comfortable than a bivvy bag on the river," Fulghum replied.

I nodded, "Just a bit noisy at times, but it keeps the rain out." Then his dinner arrived, so I returned to playing songs for the guests. That night as he left, he placed an envelope in my tip jar. Much later in the evening I counted tips and opened the envelope. It was a check for two thousand dollars. Tuition for the remainder of my early 1990's teacher college was paid.

A full week of camping-school later, I was again waiting tables and playing songs at the ranch. I stopped by Fulghum's table to thank him.

"Your help is huge, Fulghum. Thanks so much." My eyes nearly teared up with emotion.

"You're welcome, Mark. I think you'll make a great teacher when you get through, especially if you use your music."

"Hope so. I know the young ones love to sing along—you taught me that in your book." Then I changed subjects, remembering that Fulghum was adding some Anasazi First People's art to his property, including a ceremonial below-ground room. "Hey, how's the kiva coming along?"

"Almost done, just need to get some details together to make it as authentic as possible. Stop by and see it when you get time."

"I will, I will. But I've got a little something I found near the ranch that might fit the décor." My fingers slid into my pocket and felt the now so familiar conchoidal variations and sharp edges of the arrowhead. I pulled it out and opened my hand to Fulghum. "I'd like you to have it for the kiva."

His eyes sparkled, "Now that's one item I certainly do not have. Oh yes, it will fit perfectly."

Sliding the arrowhead forward onto my opened fingertips with my thumb, I handed it to Fulghum, completing our last and final trade.

There is yet another arrowhead story worth relating. It occurred during one of my early mountain bike reconnaissance trips on the White Rim of Canyonlands in about 1988, long before the explosion of popularity of the sport. A group of us were discovering the potential of this newfangled invention, the mountain bike. We were figuring out where it fit in with four-wheel drive vehicles and good hiking shoes. I had left my companions at camp earlier and cycled five miles back on the road to a spot I wanted to hike before sunset. After hiding the bike just off the road, I went for the hike. When I returned, I couldn't locate the bike.

I should have gone ahead and trampled the kryptos instead of walking on slick rock, I thought to myself as I searched for the spot on the jeep trail where I'd left the mountain bike. *Just had to be desert conscious, didn't you? Don't walk on the kryprogamic soil, stick to the Slickrock and wash bottoms. Now here I am back at the road, it's getting late, I'm hot, thirsty, tired, and on this huge flat that damned bike could be two miles in either direction. If I'd just left a few more tracks . . .*

It wasn't really a survival problem, just a major discomfort. I had already hiked seven miles round-trip overland out to the confluence of the Green and Colorado Rivers. I had also trampled plenty of cryptos well beyond the road, not worrying too much about the local biologists' precious "desert crust" they claimed was the mossy first step to turning sand into soil and took years to grow. I agreed that the crusty black growth kept sand from blowing into drifts, but I knew the stuff grew more quickly than extreme conservationists wanted people to believe. When doing a long desert hike, it was simply impossible *not* to step on some of the kryptogamic soil. Near roads and trailheads, however, I always avoided trampling it, in part out of respect for the beautiful desert gardens it harbors, and in part because I never wanted others to follow my footsteps. That almost unconscious conscience was what caused me to start my hike from the road without leaving noticeable tracks. Now back at the four-wheel drive White Rim Trail, I needed to find my mountain bike before riding another five miles back to camp where my three companions were undoubtedly starting on their second cold beer from the cooler. *Beer, hell. I need some water.* But this particular section of road ran across a five-mile flat of blackbrush, no outstanding landmarks close to the road, only the high cliffs two miles beyond rising above the flat. I had been so anxious to hike out to the overlook that I'd stashed the bike in the blackbrush carelessly. If I went the wrong way, my now thirsty hot five miles could easily turn into fifteen or more. The only consolation was that the sun was getting lower. The ninety-plus degree heat, however, would not abate for hours.

It was worth the trek, though. Before I left, my friend Carl queried, "Why the hell do you want to tromp out there in the heat? We've already covered thirty miles today, and you know you can *drive* to the Confluence Overlook from the Needles District." Carl was our sag-wagon driver. Three of us had ridden thirty miles; he had driven.

"Yes, Carl, but that's the other side of the river. That means there's two virtually insurmountable thousand-foot walls, as well as two rivers, between that jeep trail and the roadless country on this side. Plus on the other side, you look down on it from the side of one of the rivers. On this side, I'll be able to look down on it with one river on my right and one on my left, both coming together. It's kind of spiritual I guess, I just gotta see that point and feel both rivers sliding by."

"Ok, ok, I get the point," Carl shook his head. "But you better get moving; you've only got four hours of daylight left."

I left the camp and bicycled several miles back along the White Rim to a point I thought would be good for starting the hike, hid the bike in the brush, and set out.

The confluence was indeed a spiritual experience. The rivers looked still as stone, like a painting from my viewpoint on a vertical cliff a thousand feet directly above them. Both were lined in verdant green of cottonwoods, willows, tamarisk, and oak, but the muddy brown of the Colorado River where it met the clearer jade of the Green River made a striking contrast. Even from the heights, I could see the swirls of sand and jade slowly mixing together as the rivers moved inexorably down toward Cataract Canyon and Lake Powell. Wiping the sweat from my eyes, I could imagine the cool water wash over me and smell the pungent mud. I stood admiring the scene as my breathing slowed and the absolute silence of the desert surrounded me. I only stayed a few moments relishing the sight, feeling much like when reaching the summit of some remote high mountain peak, and then I started my return hike. Back in those days, I rarely carried a weighty camera with me. My memory would become the photograph of this moment.

Now here I was, two hours later, back at the jeep road looking one way, then the other, thinking. I might have discerned my bike tracks if not my footprints, but several four-wheel drive vehicles had come through during the time I was out on the plateau, obliterating any sign of my trail. I would have to guess, but before making that guess, I walked back one more time into the brush, looking for a random footprint. Surely, I had not managed to travel *entirely* on Slickrock. I sensed that I was very close to where I originally left the bike, left the road. I stopped at the edge of a large plain of stone and looked back toward the road over the slickrock terrain bedecked with blackbrush, sage, and bunch grasses. I could find no footprints. Somewhat frustrated, exhausted, thirsty and tired, I squatted down on my heels and exhaled heavily. It looked like it was going to be a late return to camp. Hope there was still some beer left. I dropped my head to my hands and let out yet another breath. As my eyes relaxed on the foreground, I noticed a shallow desert pothole filled with cryptogamic soil and a few cacti about ten feet in front of me. A subtle variation in the soils looked like a stone lodged in the soil. I moved closer and realized that I was looking at a large piece of purple and semi-translucent amber polished chert. Squatting down once again, I brushed away a tiny patch of blow sand to discover a perfectly crafted three-inch arrowhead lying flat, pointing to my left. Momentarily forgetting my parched mouth and exasperated state of body and mind, I reverently picked up the precise and beautiful artifact and examined it in wonder. It was the most finely crafted arrowhead I had ever found. Dozens of minute conchoidal indentations showed where the flintknapper had carefully worked and crafted the stone. The edges were razor sharp, and the tail had two carefully cut notches for tying. It was a perfect arrowhead, the kind every desert rat dreams of finding, but most only see in museums and in the collections of either the very lucky arrowhead hunters or the very indiscriminate ones who dig up ruins and grave sites.

Ten years of desert hiking had shown me only two other points like this one, both I found in Arches and Canyonlands National Parks. The Pack Creek arrowhead find was still many years into the future. I could still tell people where they could go find them if they were still there because I'd left them in their natural setting. I admit that one I hid a slight distance from the main trail in order to prevent it from being picked up and pocketed by the average hiker without a conscience. It had washed out of a shallow mudbank exposed by an evening thunderstorm not more than a hundred yards into a popular and heavily used trail.

After admiring this newly discovered arrowhead for a few minutes, photographing every detail of it in my mind,

I gently placed it back in its original imprint in the sand. It was so tempting to take it back to camp, maybe to take it and keep it. Still squatting on my heels, I tore my eyes away from the arrowhead and looked up. Far in the distance, a glint of silver caught my eye. I was positioned at the perfect angle to see a reflection of late sun on metal—it was the bicycle. When I stood up, the glint was gone. If I moved a foot to either side, forward or backward, the glint was gone, but not my sense of its direction. I could almost taste the cold drink of water, then a huge draught of 3.2 beer. I looked once more at the arrowhead pointing straight toward my ride to camp. Again, I picked it up and turned it over several times in my hands, memorizing it. Then I set it gently back in its imprint in the kryptos and walked to my ride.

I cycled into camp, propped the bike against the sag-wagon pickup truck and said, "Made it to the confluence overlook. Also found an arrowhead, a perfect one, 'bout so big, amber and purple chert with tie-in notches and sharp as a razor."

"Arrowhead?" asked Carl with interest. "Man, those things are worth something these days."

"Pretty amazing to find a good one," added fellow rider, Sam.

Joe cut in, "Well, let's see it, man!"

"I don't have it."

"Don't have it? What do you mean, did you lose it again?"

"Nope, I left it where I found it."

Carl wrinkled his nose and asked, "Well, where did you find it then?"

"Out there, somewhere," I returned with a sweep of my arm. "So how about a beer, any left?"

Back in the classroom, I realize my students have been writing for nearly fifteen minutes—I forgot to set the timer—and only two are off task, one sleeping, one perusing a monster truck magazine. I ask students to close their writing notebooks and get ready for a short language lesson. "Today's vocabulary-word-of-the-day is *antiquity.*"

Later on, near the end of the year, when we read Edward Abbey's essay *Rocks*, we'll talk about arrowheads, artifacts, and precious minerals—we'll also discuss ethics and greed and inscriptions and even graffiti. I might even tell students about the short time I spent with Edward Abbey as well. I'm careful, though, so my "Hayduke Lives" bumper sticker and a copy of *The Monkey Wrench Gang* both remain on my bookshelf at home. But rocks in general, I can talk about in so many ways; there is something elemental about rocks, pebbles, stones. Skipping a stone, climbing a rock, throwing rocks, gardening and landscaping, holding a gemstone, building a rock wall, carvings, sculpture, petroglyphs, pictographs—the list is long. I can also talk about rocks the extractive industries, fossil fuels, mineral trades, and dominant powers use and abuse. And then there are the magic rocks, the pet rocks, even the rock I salvaged from the excavation of my current school's new football field. It's a big, round river stone that came from ten-feet down where they were trenching for sprinkler systems and electrical conduits. Still not sure what to do with that rock, maybe turn it into a sort of painting to symbolize all the money in education spent on sports that could do so much more if devoted to the arts. And then there are polished rocks. I carry one or two with me all the time in my pocket. They make great worry stones, but more than that, they represent to me simply being grounded in nature.

Maybe next year I'll bring my little rock tumbler to school. I can already imagine giving each student a rough stone, letting them observe, feel, sketch, photograph with their phones, even weigh it. Then we would put the stones into the tumbler and let it work for six weeks or more. Each week we'd change the grit in the tumbler just like we change the focus in our learning units. When we pull out the finely polished stones, we can then connect a few concepts from English that have been equally polished.

The magic of rocks returns to class from time to time during the year. When I present Jerry Garcia's song "Ripple" we all get to ponder what he really means when he says, "Ripple in still waters, where there is no pebble tossed nor wind to blow." Paul Simon shouts strength with "I Am a Rock" and The Ozark Mountain Daredevils present faith with "Standing on the Rock." Marc Robertson even sings a song about rocks, called "Great Massive Stone." When I present Robertson's song/poem as a starter, I linger on the topics of rocks and tradition. We discuss how rocks or stones almost always figure into old stories, especially fantasy, often as symbols or talismans with magic powers. Then we discuss rock art, which leads to chalk art and the classic chalkboard from the early world of education. From there, it's a short stretch to imagining cabins, barns, hotels, schoolhouses and even whole towns built on simple stone foundations, with stone fireplaces. Stone roofs sometimes come into play. For a while, I would pull out my agate flat pick as a side note, but someone stole it. I wasn't too upset because it made an annoying clicking sound on the steel strings whenever I used it. Perhaps stone on metal needs to be reserved for things such as starting fires, architecture, jewelry, and sculpture. But what about silicates and the computer chip? Then we hit stone walls, like the one Robert Frost uses in his poem "Mending Wall," and I realize belatedly that "being stonewalled" would have made a wonderful metaphor addition to our weekly writing on the fossilized ripple rock. I make a mental note of it for next year, but I always forget. Too much to do, and too little time to do it all. Finally, I'll end the "rocks" conversation by mentioning game pieces, maybe carved stone chess figures, and leave off with a joke about how much work it would be if we had to write all our lessons on stone tablets. It all ties into Robertson's verse, "Amidst the swift currents of technology and change/We'll stand fast, like a great massive stone in the river." It all has to do with considering simplicity versus complexity—antiquity versus modernity.

Monoliths of rock and stone, in fact, are the essence of my current classroom metaphor of *The Eddy*. And then there's good old Planet Earth, the big rock we all live on. Intuitively, I knew that I needed to take home that chunk of ripple rock I found in the desert so many years ago, but I could never have dreamed how often I would use it as a tool for combining creativity, teaching, and natural inspiration.

Chapter 8: Cowboy Songs

"Horses are just like kids," explains the boss Frank Sleight, as his horse, Lacey, gives a tug on the reins he holds. He tugs back. "You gotta be firm with them, but you don't wanna be mean."

I was still more than five years away from becoming a teacher when I started adding wrangling city dudes and ranch horses to my other odd jobs at Pack Creek Ranch. It was 1990, about the year mountain biking in the desert really became the rage. The only "horse" I had ridden before was my 20th Century Stallion—a silver Stumpjumper mountain bike.

Like so many others, I thought I knew a little bit about horses and cowboys because I sang so many cowboy songs. They were a huge part of my repertoire, always crowd pleasers both on the river or at the ranch. Many years and experiences later, those same cowboy songs still capture the attention of my students, and so for about six or seven days in a row, I start class with a series of cowboy songs.

"You gotta punch 'em in the belly," continues Frank. "Otherwise they'll hold their breath until you finish cinching the strap. When they breathe again, the saddle's loose. Dudes without a sense of balance roll off with the saddle like a blob of jelly on a biscuit with too much butter under it."

I'm thinking of Marty Robbins' "El Paso" when he writes, "Though I am trying to stay in the saddle, I'm getting weary unable to ride." Despite the fact that I ultimately spent quite a bit of time in the saddle, both at the ranch and later as a volunteer trails crew worker in Yellowstone, I never carried a "Big Iron" like the one in my other favorite Robbins song, nor did I carry a rifle. But I did get to let a few horses run a time or two, and old Marty was right there by my side.

"And another thing. If you tie 'em to the rail wrong and they spook, they can break their necks. Tie 'em just like this." Frank demonstrates a releasing knot. "Now you try." I get it right after a few fumblings.

"Ok, now do it ten more times. Right now. I'll be back in a minute."

Lacey stands patiently as I hand-dance the rope around the rail again and again. I think of Jimmy Driftwood's song "Tennessee Stud" and think of how well most cowboys treat their horses. It took a true horse-lover to write, "The Tennessee Stud was long and lean/ The color of the sun and his eyes were green. / He had the nerve and he had the blood/ For there never was a horse like the Tennessee Stud." Later on, that starter song would become one of the students' favorites—probably due to all the horse sounds and hyperbole in the song, although in the back of my mind, I always suspected some kids were having other thoughts about the concept of a stud.

"Got it? Did you do it with your eyes closed?" I shake my head. "Do it now, eyes closed." I feel like a schoolboy. Frank lights up a cigarette and watches. When I'm done, he hands me the bridle. "Now let me show you how not to get bit when you put the bit in." He moves beside me and Lacey.

"First rule, no sudden moves. Second rule, let them see everything you do. Then they don't get nervous, 'cause they know what's coming, even if they don't like it much. Third rule, push gently on her nose, like this, she'll open her teeth and you slip the bit past with your hand on the outside edges." A mild smacking of horse lips and teeth ensues and the bit slides neatly into place.

"Here, you do Taylor, then Beefy, and then let's see if you can get one into Smitty. He's a bit of an asshole."

As I tie them to the rails, saddle them and bridle them, I'm recalling several more songs the guests like. "Old Cowhand" by Johnny Mercer makes me smile. Nothing like satire done cowboy style. The words come to me again, "I'm a cowboy who never saw a cow/ I never roped a steer 'cause I don't know how/ Sure ain't fixin' to start it now/ Yippie yi yo kay ee." Right now, I feel like my "legs ain't bowed, and my cheeks ain't tanned." Another song, the Stan Jones classic "Ghost Riders in the Sky" comes to mind as I tie up another horse with the slipknot. I recall, "A bolt of fear when through him/ As they thundered through the sky/ For he saw their riders ridin' hard/ And he heard their mournful cry." Frank's words resound, "One thunderclap and they'll jerk like hell." And when I walk back into the pungently fragrant tack shed, I smell the leather, the sweaty saddle blankets, the rich mixture of aromas that only happen in such a place and I think of the American folk classic, "Stewball." The words come to me as I pick another bridle from the peg, "His mane it was silver/ His bridle was gold/ And the worth of his saddle/ Has never been told." Many years later I would actually have to explain to students that horses don't really drink wine instead of water. Kids, horses, hyperbole. What a combo. But so many of the lessons I learned about wrangling horses indeed did apply to teaching kids. Fair, firm, and friendly comes to mind. Never let your guard down is another. And both understand discipline and rules—they even long for these because there is comfort in knowing what you can and cannot do. Oh yes, I musn't forget to mention that each horse, like each kid, is a completely unique challenge.

"Yup," barks Frank from behind me as on the fourth attempt I successfully get Smitty to take his bridle and bit.

"He's an asshole. Kinda like a gambler the day after he loses his stake."

Wham. Mary McCaslin's "Ballad of Weaverville" hits my memory, and I realize that I've never learned nor memorized the song. I file it away for later. I've also added some modern horse culture songs to my list over the years. Fred Small's "Heart of the Appaloosa" hits the painful and poignant side of pathos—people love the story, often with a tear in their eyes. And then there's Ian Tyson's highly romantic "Night Riders Lament" and Willie Nelson's "Don't Fence Me In." I'll probably never punch cattle, but somehow I know I'll remember my days "horsing around" at Pack Creek Ranch. But now it's time to work. The guests will be dusting their way down the path from the breakfast buffet soon. It's already getting hot—time for a sweaty trail ride, biting flies and all.

The other hired hand, Stoney, who wrangles for Jane and Ken Sleight is off today. That's why I get to work and get to start learning. Over a short period of time, I would learn much about horses, some of it the hard way. Which reminds me of another story.

Frank and Stoney could have stepped right out of the pages of a Louis Lamour or Zane Grey novel, so real were they as cowboys, and though I knew that I was worlds apart from them in both education and upbringing, there were times I wished that the tourists at Pack Creek Ranch would see me, sitting tall in the saddle, like they saw them. I had acquired the attire of an old cowboy—faded jeans, frayed western shirt, stained felt Resistol hat, hammered and dusty threadbare boots. I had learned the walk, mostly from the stiffness that everyone felt from long hours in the saddle. I had even memorized most of the local stories and learned to concoct a few tall tales of my own, yarns to spin for keeping the guests interested when the desert heat, horse sweat, and biting flies began to overpower their romantic experience. But there were two things that I discovered can never be mimicked, emulated, memorized, or impersonated. They were the look in their eyes and the expression in their voices. Of the two, Frank was the most genuine, and most experienced. But even Stoney, a three-fingered card dealer from Reno in the offseason, lived the part of Cowboy more convincingly than I ever could or ever would.

At first, I thought the big difference was that they knew horses better than I, both of them having been virtually weaned off their mothers and straight onto the backs of the creatures. Certain things would happen to me that I never believed could happen to a real cowboy. For instance, one lovely sunny day on a trail ride hosting nearly thirty city-slicker dude guests, one of my charges complained that the stirrups were maladjusted and needed to be raised. This was a common malady among city folk who generally straddled nothing bigger than their puppy dogs while hooking them up on a leash for a walk. So, I stopped the choo-choo train of horses, turned Striker around, the big black lead horse I'd chosen for the day, gave him a "I'll be right back" pat on the neck and went to work adjusting the stirrups for my guest. Striker was supposedly a superbly trained lead horse who would stand at attention when told to with reins dropped to the ground in front of him.

Just as I finished the stirrup adjustment task and got to within four feet of him, Striker snickered once, turned, and cantered away out across the pasture adjacent to the riding trail. Embarrassed, but not yet defeated, I quickly assessed the fact that running on foot was futile, and I'd have to borrow a guest's mount to retrieve him. Just as I was about to put this plan into action for my bemused guests, Stoney appeared coming out of the scrubby pinon and juniper forest on the far side of the pasture with his group of guests returning from the earlier ride. Seeing a golden opportunity to play real Cowboy and flush out his chance for some big tips, Stoney spurred Lacey, and he galloped out across the field and caught up Striker's reins, turned, and trotted him back to me. By now my face was as red as an Arizona sunset and my Western panache and pride had dropped below the elevation of Death Valley. Dudes on both sides of the field were whooping and hollering at the display of horsemanship all occurring at my expense, and Stoney grinned a tobacco-stained toothy grin at me as he handed me Striker's reins with a flourish. He drawled, "Lose somethin'?"

Several hours later, while putting tack and saddles away in the tack shed, Stoney slipped a twenty into my shirt pocket and said, "Did real good on tips today. You helped!"

"Sure," I said, somewhat dejected and still humiliated, "I helped. Or rather Striker did. Damn horse."

Then Stoney made a confession that Striker had done the same thing to him not two weeks earlier. He had managed to run after him in time and catch his reins. "Now what I do," Stoney confessed, "is I hook him up to a guest's saddle horn when I have to get off him." Maybe that's why Stoney often rode Lacey, Frank's horse, when Frank was gone despite Frank's warning that anyone who rode Lacey besides Frank was gambling with their life.

That's when I realized that horses are horses, and even the best horseman or cowboy sometimes gets pickled when dealing with them. I knew then that it wasn't just the difference in horse experience that set me apart from Stoney and Frank, but I was still trying to articulate to myself what that elemental difference was.

Frank was probably the one who inadvertently showed me, and he did it one day as we were unsaddling horses after a late afternoon trail ride. We had gotten back just in time—thunderstorms were building. A second after I finished tying the last horse to the corral rail, a sudden bolt of lightning and thunder startled all of the horses, particularly one of the horses right next to me. I still held his saddle in my arms, the stirrups bumping against my legs. He reared back, and in a snap untied the slip knot holding him to the rail with the force of his neck rising. The knot had given rather than the horse's neck, but something else happened. The end of the free-swinging lead rope twirled twice around the rail and held tight for a split second. The horse was still rearing up. In that second, the rail broke free from its post and swung out in an arc into the yard. It all happened so fast that I barely had time to flinch. The solid end of the rail missed my right temple by a hair. I felt the wind of its passing as it swooped by and landed in the dirt next to the startled horse.

Witnessing the whole thing from several yards away, Frank stiffened for a moment, then went to calm the horse. His only words were, "Good knot, anyway." Then he retied the horse and helped me pick up the downed rail. He looked me in the eye with a look that spoke volumes. If I tried to put that look into words, he might have spoken, *Sometimes the bullets miss you. Then you know you're livin' right. Today, you're livin' right. And if you hadn't tied a good release knot, the horse might also have a broken neck. That wrap around the rail, well, that's just fate.* The only three words he actually spoke during the entire ordeal were regarding the knot. Those words, "Good knot, anyway," seemed to come from his chest and ramble out of his barely moving mouth like a creak in a leather saddle. Only a cowboy could have spoken like that.

The look in his eye though, now that was something. It was one which seemed to look at me, speak much to me, and yet at the same time look out past me down across the pasture and through the valley to the thunderstorm still rumbling over the canyons ten miles away. It was a look that rivaled the Redtail hawk. He was there, and yet he was way out there somewhere. Only a true cowboy could present a gaze like that. That is when I realized that I might be a decent trail ride guide, I might become an adept horseman, I might even become a salty old storyteller, but I'd never become a true cowboy. To me, it seemed that Cowboy was something you were born into, and I had been born otherwise.

Once this realization dawned on me, it set me free from trying to be something I was never going to be and gave me a chance to focus on appreciating the rare and beautiful opportunity of spending time working with some real cowboys like Frank and Stoney. From that point on until summer ended and we all went our separate ways, I shelved the Westerns and truly lived inside a novel of my own. The catch was that this wasn't fiction; this was real life, Cowboys and all.

It's nearly impossible to impart to high school students from the city a true sense of the old West. Perhaps the closest I'll ever come is by singing them the cowboy songs. The rest will have to come from old movies, old books, stories told by old-timers, and TV reruns of *Bonanza, Magnificent Seven, High Chaparral,* and *Young Riders.*

Kids are much like horses, though, you can always lead them to water . . .

Speaking of water, something that is so special in the desert canyons, I'm reminded of yet another story from my days as wrangler for Frank, Stoney, Ken, and Jane. It's a story about a horseback trip through the watery canyon of Arches National Park named Courthouse Wash. The very last scene of this story has become somewhat of a recurring motif, even a metaphor, for the realities that face me yearly as a teacher. In essence, there might be a lot of horseshit that goes down in my classroom while I perform every kind of psychological acrobatic stunt to reach, teach, and at times control unruly and unwilling students, but when it comes time for administrators to observe class and evaluate me, well, it's no time for a rodeo. Unlike horses, I can't really knock students upside the knotty head when they misbehave and still keep my job. But students and even whole classes get out of control at times. I get tired and frequently give up a few minutes of educational time to chaos. So, I mutter and sputter and curse kids and full moons under a shallow breath and then take a deep breath and try again. All the while I'm thinking to myself, "Good God, what if an administrator stepped in for an impromptu observation right now?"

Maybe I've been lucky, but whenever principals or vice principals have dropped in, most of my ducks have been in a row, my pigeons are all in the coop, or maybe I can say my wild horses have all been corralled. That's why the absolutely honest-to-God true story I named "Courthouse Chase" comes back to me again and again. Here's what took place.

Anyone who has ever been duped by trusting the simple, honest, forthright face and deadpan serious voice of an old-fashioned cowboy giving a bit of advice will be able to appreciate this story. The cowboy was Frank Sleight, the place was Courthouse Wash in Arches National Park, the scenario was the end of a long dude ride with twenty-two French tourists, and the company of four was Ken Sleight, who was Frank's older brother and the ranch owner, Frank, myself, and my outdoorsy backcountry partner Deb Read (later to become my wife).

We had all four just completed guiding the group of tourists on horseback all the winding and colorful way up Courthouse Wash from town, and they had just departed on their big Greyhound tour bus where the bridge in Arches National Park crosses the wash about a twelve-trail ride miles up canyon from where we commenced our ride.

I might add that Frank had also just pocketed an immense roll of bills—tip money—for his superb authentic *cowboy way* head guide leadership on the ride. This was punctuated by a dazzling impromptu display of full gallop barrel racing around wash bottom willows and tamarisk on his favorite Palomino, Lacey. You see, we arrived at the bridge and pick up spot early and the busses had not yet arrived, so Frank rode us a few minutes beyond the bridge and put on his show. The French tourists loved this, especially because none of their mounts ever got past a trot throughout the ride. The one rule in trail ride guiding is *No Running!* This ensures no runaways and no lawsuits later. I must admit that even I vicariously enjoyed Frank's display, after all, he was a real born, bred, and dyed-in-the-desert cowboy. As for me, the best I could do was lean down out of the saddle and pick up my cowboy hat from the dirt and come upright on my horse again—a five-buck tip move at best.

The plan after seeing the effusive guests off on their bad smelling diesel bus—and they thought horse farts were stinky—was for Frank and Ken to load the first sixteen horses into the two trailers for the ride back to the ranch while Deb and I took the other ten mounts back down the wash where we'd meet the returning trailers a good twenty highway miles closer to the ranch, load them up, and then ostensibly split the tip and head home.

And that's where Frank offered a bit of friendly, dead-pan serious advice. "If you ride Knothead and lead, they'll all follow you just fine. No need to tie 'em all together. Not safe to do that, anyways."

Then he rode off up to the trailer on Lacey and left us to head down the canyon, me on Knothead in the front, and Deb on Smitty in the rear. Everything went as smoothly as flat water on a river trip for an entire fifty yards. But just as Deb crossed under the highway bridge, Smitty must have realized that a number of his companion dude horses were departing above him in trailers, and he wanted to be with them, not trundling back down the bug-infested, waterlogged wash behind a bunch of sweaty horses being led by a new, marginally experienced wrangler. He stopped dead. He sidestepped, he bucked, he lurched, and then Deb, being extremely agile and smart, decided that it was time to hop off and rein him in from the more stable position of standing on two feet.

I heard her call out, and I rode back to help out, and of course, the rest of the horses, seeing nothing but free country in front of them and sensing that downcanyon was the ultimate direction to home, friends, and food, began to trot friskily away from us. I figured I'd catch them in a minute, that is until Smitty saw them departing around the corner and undoubtedly thought, *Half the crew is on the trailer, the other half is going out of sight, and I'm almost all alone except for these two wranglers and old Knothead. I'm going!*

With that, he jerked the reins, which I had probably unwisely taken from Deb in an effort to calm him, out of my hands and raced off towards the other horses.

By this time we were both exasperated, and I was worried about Ken Sleight's herd of trail horses prancing down the canyon towards quicksand, suck-holes, rock ledges, and who knows what else, with no one to stop them.

Deb, who was at that time a great backcountry runner said, "Forget it, you go get the horses, and I'll just run!" Then she slipped off her riding boots and socks, flexed her bare toes, and urged, "Don't worry about me, go get Ken's horses!"

And thus began my version of a true western. After months of walking horses and guests no faster than a trot, I was finally at a full gallop, feeling the wind in my face and my heart pounding. Nobody was there to see it, let alone film it, but the memory will be carved beautifully into the desert varnish of my mind forever.

Within the first half mile of full run on Knothead, who seemed to be thoroughly enjoying a chance to air his muscles out, I thought of the mileage, the heat, and water. Quickly I unstrapped my side saddlebag, pulled out a quart bottle of water, and dropped it directly into the mud at the center of the wash hoping that Deb would "run across it" and have drinkable water. One glance back told me that it was quite visible, and so I urged Knothead into a relaxed gallop and began to wonder where I would find the horses.

I caught sight of Beefy, the rear horse in the frolicking group, about three miles downcanyon, and by the time I caught sight of the leader, I could see that it was Smitty. Nonetheless, they were not traveling much past a canter, and so after another quarter mile of narrow trail through the brush, I began passing horses as the wash widened and I headed for the front. That's when Smitty decided that this was a race. I might well have let him go, knowing that the canyon ended at the river and they probably would all stop there, but several treacherous suck-holes and rock ledges lay between, and I just didn't trust Smitty's judgment anymore. So, I urged Knothead into a full gallop. Smitty shook his head as if to say, "I don't have to carry a rider, nah-na-na-na-nah-nah nah!" The race was on, and fortunately, a sandy wide stretch of canyon bottom lay ahead of us.

Knothead was Ken's personal mount and riding him at full gallop, I could appreciate why. He was fast, and he was smooth, and he seemed to be having more fun than ever, yet was determined, as I, to win the race. Just before beating Smitty, I distinctly recall having the feeling that we were flying, that I was really a cowboy or a Native, or even perhaps a member of Genghis Khan's youthful gang sailing across the Asian Steppes in a moment of pure excitement, energy, and exultation. I laughed and whooped, and then we caught Smitty, headed him towards the wash bank and slowed him to a stop.

I immediately grabbed his reins, feeling lucky that he hadn't stepped on them and taken a tumble, tied them up, untied his lead rope, which was still on the saddle, (we always left them on for Dude rides,) and firmly led him towards the other horses that were still trotting in our direction. One by one, I began gathering up the nine other horses and tying them into a string, looping lead-ropes over saddle horns.

My plan was to tie everyone up to a huge juniper tree nearby, then return to retrieve Deb who was now running the eight or so miles that lay between where I was and our starting point at the bridge.

I don't remember exactly which horse was the last to gather up, but I lucidly recall the look in his eye that said, "That running was fun! I'm goin' back to do it again!" And with that, he bolted up canyon. I knew that Knothead had had enough and was sweating, but fortunately not lathering, so I tied all the other horses up in a hurry, him included, and jumped on Striker in hopes of catching my next runaway before he ran all the way back to the bridge. Of course, Deb was coming down, and she probably would stop the horse, even ride him on down. But by this time, it was a matter of pride, for *by God I was going to bring Ken's horses back in style or I was going to die trying!*

Striker was certainly willing, even shaking his head as we began to gallop. He, too, seemed to enjoy the run. Fortunately, his run was not as long. I found the stray horse two miles up canyon, standing hoof deep in the water wondering where everyone had gone to. He neighed at our approach and trotted towards us. I grabbed his lead rope and we cantered back in the direction of the other horses. All the while I was praying that they were still there since I knew all too well the propensity for dude horses to find a way to become untied from any mooring. They were all there, resting in the shade like nothing had happened.

By the time I sorted out the string of wayward mounts, found another water bottle for a drink, and got ready to ride again, Deb appeared, running strong at the end of her eight or maybe even nine-mile trek, boots in one hand, water bottle in the other. *No wonder she summited Denali* I thought smiling as I greeted her amidst my throng of sweaty horses.

She smiled and said, "That was a *Great* run. Thanks for the water!"

I smiled back and related my escapades. She just laughed and then commented, "You ride, I want to run the rest, then I can say I ran the entire thing!" And so she did, except for the last 100 yards.

We both rode smoothly and calmly up the last leg of trail towards the highway fence and gate where Frank and Ken were sipping on something cool and waiting for us. All of the horses were calmly following, tied neatly in a lead-rope row, and Deb was riding Striker in the rear. Frank nodded in approval, I nodded back, and we loaded up the horses and headed home to the ranch. The last thing I remember was Ken patting Knothead on the cheek saying, "Did you enjoy the ride old buddy?"

When I sing cowboy songs as starters for my students, I am overwhelmed by my own memories of my brushes with cowboy culture. Yet I think experiences like our Courthouse Chase helped prepare me for herds of kids, with all their quirks, unpredictability, and lovability. When dealing with horses, you have to keep cool, expect the unexpected, and learn how to keep things moving, sane, and safe. And often, when administrators look for the impossible, you have to put on a great show, just like Deb and I did with Ken's horses so long ago as we came out of Courthouse Wash.

Chapter 9: Running a River of Words

"Welcome to Café 22!" The students look at me, puzzled. Some glance at the clock, but it's nowhere near lunchtime. I can see them thinking, *What's he getting at?*

"Yep, you are in a small café now. We might be in France or San Francisco, or Italy, or somewhere in an island village. We might be in downtown Salt Lake City, just a few miles away. But it's always the café. Café 22."

I wait. Finally, a hand timidly rises. "Why a café? Why the number 22?"

"Ever notice that this room is a full ten feet shorter than any other room on the second floor of this school? See how crammed-in our forty desks are? Intimate, isn't it? Just like a café. And what do people do in a café? They talk about things like stories and novels and poetry and current events and life in general, just like we will do all year long. But *this* Café 22 is not located in a big city; it's located in a small town next to a national park. Which means that customers also talk about hiking and parks and wilderness and wildlife and conservation as well as books and authors."

Students are bemused. "So why the number 22?"

"What is our room number?"

"It's 222."

"That's what the new plastic room number signs glued to the old brick walls say. But what do the classic 1950's brass numbers on the door say? John, go take a look."

John, who sits in desk number one next to the door goes out into the hall for a moment, then returns. He smiles, "It says 22. The third 2 is missing, but you can see the outline of it on the old wooden door."

"Welcome to Café 22!"

Metaphors are the umbrella that shades the blinding sun of boredom from my head, that protect me from the downpour of mediocrity, and even designate my own special place on the crowded beach of teaching. For some reason, I didn't need metaphors while teaching small classes in rural Utah. Maybe the close proximity of relatively unpeopled wild places was enough to keep my spirit alive while under the roof of the school. When I moved into the urban world of teaching, and my classes routinely neared or exceeded forty students, I needed extra inspiration, extra humor, extra something. So, I started using metaphors to describe my classrooms, and by extending that metaphor I began to play with creative ideas and with students' heads.

After four years working at Café 22, we moved out of town for a year. When we returned, I signed on at a new school, and this time I landed in a beautiful big room. But the room was located in the center of the building—windowless. No amount of posters on the walls could make up for the absence of natural light from the outdoors. And when the power went out, total darkness ensued. During one dark power-outage, I could imagine seeing the Milky Way in the ceiling. Then I saw the metaphor.

"Welcome to the C-211 Wilderness," I said as each new class began. "Room C-211 is located in the center of the school, as far away from the windows as you can get. So, what is Utah about as far away from as you can get in America?"

"Good drivers?" someone responds. We all laugh.

"It's about as far away from the oceans as you can get. You see, we are the American interior wilderness. Imagine being in Utah in the 1700's through the 1800's. Imagine how far away the sea and all the culture of the coastal cities would be at that time. Maybe that's why to this day Utah consists of nearly seventy percent public lands including five national parks and seven national monuments. We'll learn about all of that, read and write about it as well as the evolution of American literature here in the C-211 Wilderness."

Five years later, a room with windows became available, and I had earned five years' worth of seniority. The room was located on the second floor and was the second room back from the stairs that led down to the main entrance, the auditorium, and the office. But the new room needed a new metaphor, and that's where the idea for The Eddy came from. When you were released from my room at the end of class or the end of the day, you were swept up in a rush of over 2,000 students headed down the waterfall stairs toward the front doors. When you were in my room, sometimes it seemed like the world was passing you by on its way to somewhere else.

"Welcome to The Eddy," I began. "Can anybody tell me what an eddy is?" If I'm lucky, one student will be a fisherman or have run a river and know.

"Usually an eddy is a safe place to park on a river, though some eddies can be quite dangerous. When we're in a good eddy, not only are we parked safely watching the river go by, but sometimes we'll even go upstream, against the current. And as your guide, I'll point out things along the banks of the river that you might not notice while flying downstream."

Students look at me, somewhat dumbfounded. *Is this guy for real?*

"But eddies occur not only in rivers, they also occur in the ocean, the atmosphere, in a windstorm or a snowstorm or a lava flow or a glacier. And eddies happen in literature, history, culture, and society. The universe is full of eddies, and so our universe this year is, quite simply, The Eddy."

I see a few nods and smiles from students who "get" the concept of the extended metaphor. *Readers,* I think to myself. The rest of the students file out of class looking somewhat bemused. But when I start the next class with the same metaphor, and the next, and the next, they begin to understand.

"As soon as we hit the eddy today, I looked around the boat and noticed a few loose ropes. That won't do. We could lose gear, or worse yet, someone could get tangled up in those ropes in a rapid and get pulled under. The first loose rope is attached to our hall pass . . ."

Teaching indeed reminds me of running a river with a boat full of diverse passengers, some enjoying the trip, some hating the trip, and some mutinously bent on sinking the boat. Oh yes, there are also two or three who have inevitably jumped out and are floating aimlessly alongside. Yet the teacher in the twenty-first-century classroom must persevere in guiding everyone through a wilderness that is often much more complex and dangerous than the real outdoors.

I'm reminded of one great year when my school offered creative writing for a year, and they gave me the job of teaching it. Instructing creative writing, however, takes this wilderness river trip downcanyon and into the rapids where everything about teaching changes dynamically. Suddenly everyone is charged with adrenaline and soaked with splashes of insight, imagination, and the sometimes too cold slap in the face of that ominous blank page.

In creative writing class, the learners who previously enjoyed the standard education trip guided by teaching are now usually cheering with delight at the stimulation of the writing river's rapids. The learners who were hating the ordinary education trip, if they made it this far, are now usually hanging on for dear life, yet quite interested now in the trip if only for reasons of self-preservation.

And if any of the mutinous members of the normal teaching river trip managed to stay aboard and make it into creative writing class, well, they're usually blown away by the power and force of the river, the unimaginable skill of the river guide, and the amazing ability of the rest of the crew to work together bailing, high siding, punching waves, and cheering each other on through the immense roar of the powerful river. If poems, essays, and stories were water, the overwhelming beauty of the calm stretches and the explosive power of the rapids can move the mutineer to tears, can bring them back to the vistas of being a learner.

What about the two or three who jump overboard and swim away from normal education? They are probably sitting on the rocks beside the river, wondering at the fun everyone seems to be having as the crew sails on by, secretly envious of the whole trip.

Snapshots taken from each different guided trip through a creative writing class inevitably remain in the instructor's (or guide's) mind for years to come. A phrase, a word, a poem, a story, a great hook, a memorable image all make each trip of teaching this subject unforgettable. But memory sometimes fades, and the pictures begin to run together like a giant watercolor painting of a glorious sunset in the canyons—you know, the kind where silhouetted ridges and mesas recede into ever-changing hues of horizon, air, and cloud.

That's where the literary magazine comes in. It's more like a snapshot of memories these days, often being literally given away in hopes of capturing some soul's attention. But once they are captivated, readers often sign up for the trip and join the river. I think of the literary magazines I've helped writing classes publish over the past ten years and realize that we've had some great trips together. Teaching makes me write more myself—after all, the guide must remain strong in case someone on the journey needs a hand! I also realize that throughout the years, many of my own essay ideas have come from moments when I've wanted to show the sights to my students, my boatload of river runners, who are along for the trip. For instance, one day in a pique of creativity I stepped off the boat, walked into the nearby woods, and scrawled into the air as if onto a great chalkboard what I was seeing. I urged the others to see it likewise. I spoke and wrote, *There was a whisper, a subtle voice in the wind, which became a river of unspoken language coursing ceaselessly through the great majestic old growth timber. The huge and magnificent trees, giants of the primal forest, became the swaying, singing chorus within nature's voice, uttering a great collective sigh.* Then I teased my charges by saying, "You might also note that I have a predisposition to prepositions, and often pause for appositives!!"

It must have been the English teacher in me coming out. After all, if words are the air inflating the river trip rafts, then grammar is the oars which propel it! Take the metaphor deeper. If imagination is the canyon, then the words and writing become the river.

Yes, I would agree that this essay is overboard with metaphors, slopping with similes, and gushing with idealism. Yet immersion is the nature of river trips.

And so, I continue to teach, to write, and to guide. My feet are always metaphorically wet, and the river runs ever free. Perhaps it's the latent guide in me that compels me to stop class and ask students to listen and smell whenever it rains. I've even done this from a classroom with no windows when the muffled sound of thunder alerted me to the storm. When silence fell upon the class, we could hear the pouring rain through the roof of the building. Ah, rain, what a wonderful force. And now I'm remembering one particularly poignant rainstorm that called me and one of my students out of the building and into the spring.

It was March, and I was inside the media center of a modern high school, tabulating results, pushing ballots, and monitoring my students' progress. I was the debate coach, and it was state tournament. One of my debaters was good. So good, in fact, that she had qualified for nationals during her first year. This was her second year, and it looked like she was going to win the state championship in Extemporaneous Speaking. She had scored first place in all four rounds of speaking; there was just one round to go.

Earlier in the day, I had heard a noise coming from the library skylight high above and paused to realize that rain was pattering on the roof. Constraints of the tournament—things that had to get done, judges to assist, ballots to record, students to help out—all kept me chained to the school, but my heart broke free and was wandering around outside of the building in the thunderstorms. They were the first thunderstorms of the spring after a very long and cold and snowy winter. I wanted to be out there with my heart.

But the team was doing well, and Tesch, my young extemporaneous speaker just might win, and so might a few other of my promising debaters. So I worked. Finally, I saw a break in the debate action coming and knew it was time to check on my students—see how they were doing. I went out onto the mezzanine overlooking the commons and headed downstairs. Again, it took restraint to aim for my students and not for the door outside to the rain. They were waiting for me, all with stories to tell and questions to ask about where they might place at the state tournament. But Tesch was not there! My extemporaneous speaker was nowhere to be seen. When I asked, one student said, "Oh, Tesch felt like she melted down in final rounds and was really upset. She blasted right past us in tears. Don't know where she is now."

Uh oh. Time for some of the other kind of coaching. And so, I began roaming the vast halls of the modern school looking for her. Passing one long hallway with exterior doors at the end of it, I caught a glimpse of her walking past the doors. She was outside! I sprinted for the doors.

The rain had momentarily stopped between squalls and there were even some patches of blue sky shining through the clouds. It was cool and fresh, but not cold. But the thing that really hit me was the smell—first rain of the spring. I took one long deep and glorious breath, then set out around the corner to catch my student.

By the time I strolled hurriedly up next to her, I could see that she had been crying but was getting it together. We walked along the front of the school while she explained what had transpired. The champion had indeed melted down, which meant she would probably get second place instead of first. She told me in a disheartened voice that she deserved fifth place or even no place at all. I could see that she was very discouraged. Time for damage control, time for that pep talk I give all of my high school students when they feel like this moment was the most important moment of their lives. It was time to again discuss the fact that high school is nothing more than simply a blip on the radar screen of life. It doesn't even rate a lightning strike. College might do that, but not high school.

I said, "Tesch, stop walking for a minute. Look around. Take a deep breath. Smell this air! Look at those debaters over there in the courtyard. They're frolicking like ponies, debate is the furthest thing from their minds right now. And you know why?"

She looked sideways at me, puzzled.

"Just think, it's the *first rain of the spring*, and you are out smelling it! This is an important moment. You wouldn't have appreciated this magnificent moment if you had nailed your speech, because you wouldn't have been upset enough to go walking outside alone in the rain! Things happen for a reason. We'll discuss the reasons in a sec, but right now, think about being in this rain-drenched and richly beautiful moment. This little space is as important as anything right now, maybe more important than anything."

It certainly diverted her attention. Then I added, "Just imagine being a frog right now. How important would your speech on sub-prime mortgages be to a frog?"

She laughed. "Not very important I guess."

"Exactly, but this rain? This humidity? Ahh, now there's something that can change the world. And you and I are here to appreciate it. Think about this. Scientists are now saying that frogs are disappearing at an alarming rate. That it bodes ill for the environment. They are the proverbial canary for the coal mine of earth's environment. To me, that supersedes mortgages. Might even make them a moot point."

She laughed.

"Now let's take this one step further. You know what serendipity is right?"

"Yes, happy accident. Something that you just happen upon that is really good, especially in science." Smart kid, nice to have smart kids who remember previous lessons.

"Good. So, think of this moment, smelling the new rain, as serendipity. If you had aced that speech, you'd be gloating to your teammates, basking in the glow of an almost certain first place tournament trophy. Never would you have fled your peers to seek solace beyond the building doors. Now let's go into the future. You're certain to get an environmental topic again soon. Maybe it will be at a national tournament, more important even than State! Those types of topics happen all the time, right?"

Her head tilted slightly, not quite sure what I was up to. "Yes, I think the green movement is here for a while."

I continued, "Ok, and you want to add humor to your speeches whenever possible also, right?"

"Right. It sure makes the judges connect with me. I think it's really neat to put some humor into serious topics. Makes people remember things."

"Correct. So now take this bombed speech moment, go forward in time, you are speaking on an environmental topic, serious stuff, and you pause and say, 'Frogs, yes that's right, frogs—let me focus on frogs for a minute. How about a croak as a form of speech? Those funny little bellowing slimy warty green things that make kids in the swamp on a science field trip squeal with delight when they catch one. Frogs.' Then you make the point, maybe you state, 'What's more important, mortgages or the environment? What's more important, driving your car every day five times a day, or being able to smell clean air?' You'll have a winning speech, humor and all. Because of your failure today, you just might have gained a key to success for tomorrow."

She smiled again.

I then asked, "Did I make you forget your last speech for a moment?"

"Yes, for a moment."

"Well, that's a well spent moment. Take another breath of this wonderful air, and then I've got to get back in and finish this tournament up. Try not to dwell on your speech. Are you ready to go cheer some of your teammates on? Katie and Alex are finalists in Public Forum, they might take the championship!"

"Yes, I'm ready. Thanks for talking me down."

Katie and Alex did win the championship. Tesch took second place but later went on to qualify for nationals, many times. Kept winning awards throughout her senior year. Became team captain. Might actually have put frogs into a future speech for all I know. Her event was Political Extemporaneous Speaking, so in spite of needing the necessary sources and analysis, there was always room for creative, even metaphorical flair. Sometimes, I wish that we recorded those speeches, but alas, only the speaker and the judge ever heard the originals. Tesch most likely didn't recall the specifics of her second-place state speech, but I believe she will remember that moment just after the rain; and as time often does, that brief experience will become a long and lasting memory.

The rain, the snow, the wind and sun and seasons all have a place in my teaching. Inspiration flourishes often by simply looking out the window at the weather, or else it arises in the transcendental imagery of the poetry, the wild motif in the story, the storm of the novel's heart, the ecology of the nonfiction. And the extended metaphors of the wilderness, the eddy, even the café (with its outdoor seating of course) flow on like a great river of words.

Chapter 10: Yellowstone Summer and Wolves

I have a striking watercolor painting of a wolf on my classroom wall. It was given to me many years ago by one of my students who excelled in art. Every time I look at that painting, I recall one summer that I spent working in Yellowstone—it was the summer when wolves were first reintroduced to the park. Every time I look at that painting, I dream that someday I'll see a wolf in the wild. I was working in a different corner of the park when they released the first wolves that were imported from Canada. My then soon-to-be wife was lucky enough to glimpse one of them that summer on one of her ranger patrols, but all I saw was the ordinary menagerie of grizzly bears, elk, moose, black bear, coyotes, sandhill cranes, swans, herons, eagles, hawks, deer and a bunch of other Yellowstone locals.

Deb recounts, "I was patrolling the high country above Bechler, on the trail toward Norris. I was giving my horse a break by walking for a spell, and I had taken off those hot riding boots and was walking for a few minutes in the lush green grass where the trail ran through the high meadows. That's when I met up with the South Entrance district ranger. He was on horseback as well. I let Chubby, my ever-so-reliable patrol horse, graze for a minute while we talked. I mentioned that the ground felt actually hot under my feet. He commented that this area was like that, despite being so far from the nearest hot spring. After a minute I felt that tickly feeling in my neck, looked out across the meadow, and saw movement. 'I think we're being watched' I said to the other ranger. He simply gazed out, nodded, then pulled his binoculars from his saddlebag and handed them to me, not saying a word. *That's not a coyote,* I thought as I gazed through the lenses. She was beautiful, black tan and gray, with a black face. I handed the binoculars back to my fellow ranger and said simply, 'Time for me to be getting back.' The wolf reintroduction in Yellowstone had not been publicized yet, and I sensed that he was tracking this wolf. I kept his secret, and I knew he trusted that I would do so. Not unlike wolves, there was an unwritten communication between us as rangers, between us as passionate lovers of wild places and wild things."

When students ask me if I've ever seen a wolf, I point to the painting and say, "Every day." Then I explain to them that I don't absolutely have to see a wolf in order to make my life complete, but that I believe our natural world must retain wolves in order for it to be complete. Ever since I worked that summer in Yellowstone, I've followed the wolf story, and I've found a way to bring the subject of wolves into the classroom. *Canus Lupus* first made its way into my teaching when, very late in life, I got around to finally reading Aldo Leopold's *A Sand County Almanac.* It was actually a high school student who quoted Leopold as an epigram on one of her essays that reminded me that Leopold was an important author, especially for someone who loves the outdoors. I was already curious about this author who was so often quoted on Sierra Club Wilderness calendars and BLM kiosk signs. I bought a copy one day while still teaching in rural Utah and read it on some of the eternal bus rides to distant schools for debate competitions. By mid-book, I approached my principal and got permission to buy a class set of the book for my AP students. The wolf was here to stay. And with the wolf came the lions and bears and eagles and cranes and virgin timber and... well, somebody should have thumped me over the head with Leopold's book much sooner in life. Now I could make connections between American conservation beginning with Henry David Thoreau, moving into Aldo Leopold, on to Rachel Carson, and then ending with any number of modern writers like Barry Lopez, Wallace Stegner, Al Gore, or E.O. Wilson.

Later on, I purchased a class set and even a copy of the book for every student in all of my honors level English classes at two other schools. The book is still required reading for my current IB students. At some point in time during the process of chasing good materials to teach, I realized that I'm as good as a publicity agent when it comes to promoting and selling certain books. Twice I've "sold" upwards of 200 copies of Rachel Carson's *Silent Spring,* and three times in a row, I "sold" 100 or more copies of Aldo Leopold's' *A Sand County Almanac.* Who were the buyers? Ah, there's the rub. They were four different unsuspecting school districts who approved the purchases for education, almost sight unseen. You see, when it comes to book approval, nonfiction texts usually required none. I probably could have procured Edward Abbey's *Desert Solitaire* this way as well, but like the wolf, I know how to stay out of the gun sights and retreat quietly. For Abbey, I settled for copying a strictly legal "class set" of his essays "Rocks" and "Water."

My 1993 summer clearing trails in Yellowstone and assisting my soon-to-be wife, who was a full backcountry ranger, not only gave me a front seat to the wolf reintroduction, but it also made me aware of generational responsibility in American culture. Earlier generations *made* Yellowstone and all the other national parks *possible*—the political leaders, the thinkers, the writers, the artists, and photographers, many of whom I would later draw upon for their work and words and images when teaching English. What was I going to do to ensure that these wonders of the national parks and other wilderness areas remained for future generations? I thought to myself, *I'm not rich, some years it's hard to pay membership dues to Sierra Club and Wilderness Society. I'm not a politician. I'm not widely published, though I'd love to be. I'm just a simple English teacher.* Driving back from Yellowstone to embark on my second year of teaching high school English, and not certain I really wanted to deal with the hassle of teaching high schoolers in general, I started to think about the history of conservation in America, and I realized that education was where I *could* make a contribution to the future. All I had to do was to share my passion for wild things and wild places. Add a little creativity, let some wolves loose in the wilderness of my own mind, and the magic of imagination could happen.

"Did you read the article on wolves?" Deb asks me as she sets the copy of *High Country News* on top of my leaning pile of tenth-grade writing notebooks.

"Wolves? Yellowstone involved?"

"Yep. But you won't like it."

"Uh-oh." I open the monthly periodical, which is published in Colorado and is focused largely on conservation and environmental issues in the West, and read an essay from the syndicated "Writers on the Range" page of the periodical. The writer, Bryce Andrews, is working for a ranch in Montana which is adjacent to Yellowstone National Park. He explains in detail how he and others were forced to kill wolves that had strayed from the park and started feeding on cattle. His essay is titled, "Living precariously with wolves and cattle."

I read the essay, and though I completely understand that wolves, bears, mountain lions, and other wildlife sometimes must be killed in order to protect human interests, there is something about this particular essay that rankles seriously.

I stop short at this passage Andrews has penned, "I thought about Aldo Leopold's famous line about a fierce green fire in a wolf's eye, and I wanted to see it die."

"He misquoted Leopold!" I exclaim to Deb. "People who haven't read Leopold will get exactly the opposite impression of his view on wolves!"

"He also writes like he enjoyed killing the wolves," Deb replies.

"Yeah, not the tone to take," I reply. Then I read the essay for a second time—this time with a highlighter. *I'm going to write a letter on this one* I think to myself.

Andrews' essay appeared in one of the August issues of the paper. My letter was printed by September. Whenever I discuss the importance of properly quoting or alluding to authors, I bring out both the essay and my response and we read them as a class. But before we do, we all reread Leopold's classic essay from *A Sand County Almanac* "Thinking Like a Mountain."

Here's what I wrote in response to that 2007 essay:

Wolf Lit 101

Bryce Andrews not only misrepresented Aldo Leopold in his "Living precariously with wolves and cattle" (*HCN, 8/20/07),* but he also failed to acknowledge the other side of the public lands grazing issue: Many of us would rather have wolves and healthy rangelands than cattle.

Leopold's famous essay "Thinking Like A Mountain" from *A Sand County Almanac* adroitly identifies the issue of how much the loss of the wolf has cost us. Andrews paraphrases the line "fierce green fire in a wolf's eye" completely out of context and incorrectly. Perhaps he should join my AP Literature course back in high school for a refresher. I teach that essay as one of the most compelling persuasive pieces ever written in defense of the wolf—cow kills and all. When Leopold watches the wolf's light expire, he realizes with belated epiphany that ". . . there was something new to me in those eyes—something known only to her and to the mountain."

And so that leaves us with the issue of public lands. Are not these everyone's lands as well as the rancher's? When a rancher kills a wolf, he is killing part of our inalienable rights. He is killing a vital check and balance we are trying to reestablish before it's too late for land and wildlife health. And oh yes, I forgot to ask, how much money did we, the government, reimburse this rancher for all of his slaughtered cattle?

I am reminded of the mentality portrayed in Nicholas Evans' *The Loop*. The problem is, this isn't fiction. This type of wolf killing is not responsible, nor is the writing. Hopefully, Bryce Andrews will have time to reread Leopold when he begins his grad school program in environmental studies, maybe the second time around he'll truly understand it.

Mark Doherty
Salt Lake City, Utah

Since incorporating this discussion of wolf rhetoric, I've had three students give me original wolf paintings. My favorite, the watercolor painting, watches over my classroom at all times. She's part of our wilderness, she's discussed at the tables of the outdoor café, and we see her when we pause in an eddy on the river and scan the far walls of the canyons.

Chapter 11: Rhythm and the Tides

"How do you officially end a sentence thought in writing? What punctuation mark?" I query.

"A period," several students respond immediately.

"Right, but what about a semicolon? What does a semicolon do?"

One student timidly answers, "It connects two sentences?"

"Right again. So, what is the difference between a period at the end of a sentence and a semicolon at the end of a sentence?" I wait a long three count. "Kaylee, any guesses?"

"Um, a semicolon means you have more to say?"

"Yes, that's good. A semicolon connects sentences with linking or related thoughts or ideas. They keep the message moving, rather than ending the thought—period."

I can see students wondering, *So what's your point? We were reading this weird Poe story and you suddenly stopped for a grammar lesson?*

But "Masque of the Red Death" is a perfect example of prose that is punctuated in a way that emulates and enhances the scene. Poe's initial descriptions of the great Ebony grandfather's clock and its chiming and his description of the unstoppable movement of the masked mummer—The Red Death—through the seven chambers are both written with extended syntax that doesn't stop with a period until final impact has been attained.

"Ok, now put your finger on the words *Its pendulum swung*. . . I won't stop reading until I reach a period—a final closing to the next thought process Poe presents." I begin to read, but I don't stop until I hit the words *reverie or meditation* 19 lines and 139 words later.

"Look at how far away the beginning of this series of clauses began. Why didn't Poe use a period?"

"Because he's a complicated guy?"

"Funny, Jake, and probably partly true, but let me ask you this, what is onomatopoeia?"

John answers, "It's when a word sounds like what it's describing, like snap or click or whoosh."

"Yes. So now apply the idea of onomatopoeia to punctuation and the situation the masked mummers are in at the Prince's ball when the clock chimes. Ever heard the chimes of a floor-to-ceiling grandfather's clock? Bong, Bong, Bong . . . you can't hear anything else. And if it chimes nine, ten, eleven or even twelve times . . . I call this onomatopoeic prose. The literal structure of Poe's words and sentences emulate the scene in the story. Nothing can stop or overpower the loud chiming of the great ebony clock in Poe's story, not even punctuation that employs periods. Think I'm kidding huh? Just wait until a scene at the *end* of this story. Again, I have students place a finger on the words *But from a certain nameless awe* . . . and I don't stop until *been made to arrest him.* The passage lasts for 17 lines and 123 words.

I ask, "Why no periods here? What's happening?"

"Nobody wants to stop the crazy guy, the Red Death."

"Right! So, Poe has him travel all seven of the rooms without a period to stop him. And what room does the Red Death character finally stop in?"

"The black velvet one," answers one student.

"That's right! So, imagine the punctuation mark of a period as a complete pause in the action, whereas a semicolon or a comma or a dash keeps the action moving.

When the clock chimes, when the Red Death moves, there is nothing to stop either.

I know then, they get it.

Not long after reading Poe, we tackle several genres of essay. I've picked Rachel Carson's opening chapter "The Marginal World" from her book *The Edge of the Sea* which is printed in full by the thoughtful creators of our classic 1986 literature textbook. I pause early in the essay, remind the students of Poe's punctuated clock and the Red Death monster and instruct them, "As I read this passage, think about what Carson is doing with commas and phrasing."

Occasionally a swell, stronger than the rest, rolled smoothly over the rim and broke in foam against the cliff. But the intervals between such swells were long enough to admit me to the ledge and long enough for a glimpse of that fairy pool, so seldom and so briefly exposed.

Very few students get this one, so I pause and explain, "Carson's phrases, *short, short, strong medium, long phrase, then short* come at us *just like the swells at low tide!* I can always see a few heads nodding in agreement, and I know they are lucky students who have visited the magical world of the oceans and tide pools at least once during their young lives.

"So let's go back to that passage we read written by Emily Carr at the beginning of the year when she was describing the coastal Indian village and the beach." I put the passage on the projector screen,

Skedans Beach was wide. Sea-drift was scattered over it. Behind the logs the ground slipped up a little to the old village site. It was smothered now under a green tangle, just one grey roof still squatted there among the bushes, and a battered row of totem poles circled the

bay; many of them were mortuary poles, high with square fronts on top. The fronts were carved with totem designs of birds and beasts.

"Look at the phrasing, it's just like waves washing onto the beach. Or you could look at the syntax where the first four sentences get progressively longer, like the tide coming in." I pause to let this sink in, thinking about how I myself would so love to have seen what Carr did in the 1940's along the Vancouver, BC Coast.

For the benefit of those who need an example of onomatopoeic prose closer to home, I also stop while reading Edward Abbey's essay "Water" from *Desert Solitaire*.

"Hey," I exclaim right in the middle of my reading, "Do you remember Poe's crazy punctuation in "Masque of the Red Death? Or how about Rachel Carson's phrases that ran like waves in her essay? Here's one by Abbey. Watch how the phrases, the commas, and the preposition all create the image."

The water oozes from the grasp of moss to fall one drop at a time, one drop per second, over a lip of stone.

Later in the essay, I point out how Abbey drops the conventions of dialogue writing—no quotes et al—in order to emulate two friends communicating just by looking at each other rather than actually speaking. I read to them:

What was all the bellowing about? I wanted to know. I'm sorry, he said, but it's a horrible way to die. Get out of that mud, I said, and let's get out of here. It ain't just mud, he said. I don't care what it is, get out of there; you look like an idiot. I'm sinking, he said.

"So does Abbey not know how to write proper dialogue?" No answers. "Turn to the beginning of the essay; see the dialogue conventions being used? Why doesn't he use them later with this rather funny conversation with his friend Newcomb?"

Sharper students quickly grasp the concept of formal dialogue versus implied dialogue; they also begin to understand nuances of creative nonfiction. Someday I will be reading their onomatopoeic prose when a few of them become writers. Meanwhile, I keep looking for more examples, and I even attempt to write a few of my own. Inspired by Carson, I penned this paragraph a while back, all the while imagining the constant yet syncopated rhythm of the waves along the Pacific Coast:

Early risers, storm goers, and people who gravitate to places where there are few other people, are always treated by a world of voices without words. They are treated to a world of smells without cooking. They are treated to the taste of the sea air, the salt on fingertip. They are treated to the tickling of sand washing under toes and feet, and in northern climes to the sweetly aching chill on the ankles, thighs, of icy fresh seawaters. In warmer climes, the feel of salt water caressing the skin. So many sights, sounds, scents, and tastes—all of which are diminished by noisy company. Even when Deb and I travel the sands together, long periods of vocal silence punctuate our time. We are listening to the concert of the sea, and it seems impertinent and impolite to speak in human terms at times. The birds call, the wind sings, the rocks crackle with barnacles, the surf hisses, gurgles, splashes, gulps, spills—and the breakers respond with thunderous applause. Who needs human voices? I have not the temerity to suppose my sounds are better.

After a while, students who read a lot start coming to me with their own examples of authors using prose in onomatopoeic fashion. When that happens, we applaud creativity at its finest and I savor the moment.

All these passages and writings about the ocean make me want to run off to the beach to smell the salt air, feel the chilly pacific numb my ankles, and hear the rolling thunder of the waves. Whenever possible, most often in the spring, we do exactly this, despite the distance and the travel expense. And to warm up for the trip, I always time my writing topic of seashells for a week or two before departure. It only takes a few sand dollars, a jar full of mixed snail shells, and a couple of seashell necklaces to get students out of their Utah comfort zone and make them ponder the coasts.

"Ok, first write down this quote," I speak the quote as I scrawl it on the board, *The edge of the sea is a strange and beautiful place. Rachel Carson.* Then I wave Carson's book *The Edge of the Sea* around as I hold a seashell necklace in the other hand. "Let's talk seashells."

I pull a few polished Dove shells and Dog Whelks out of an ancient cigar box and pass them around the class. "What can we say about seashells? What can we do with them? What can we make out of them?"

I wait for a minute, and if I'm lucky, Class Clown holds one up to his ear and says, "Hey, I can hear the ocean."

"Oh grow up," says Clown's friend.

I smile, "Well if you can't really *hear* the ocean, you certainly can *imagine* it can't you?"

Then Smart Kid raises a hand. "How about musical instruments, like hand shells dancers use or the conch shell that the boys find in *Lord of the Flies*?"

"Ahh, now we're getting somewhere." I scrawl the words *musical instruments—conch shells, castanets, drums.*

"Castanets are what the pair of hand shells dancers use are called. And some islanders use large open shells to spread skins over to make drums. With a little research, we might find several other musical instruments made from shells."

Then I walk over to the guitar hanging on the wall and hold it up, "Speaking of musical instruments and shells, what parts of many traditional acoustic instruments are made from seashells?"

Usually, I have to point to the headstock and fingerboard of the guitar. "What do you call these?"

"Inlays," calls out Woodshop Kid.

"Righto!" Mother of pearl in older instruments, abalone in newer instruments. This guitar has abalone."

Soon we get to jewelry, mobiles, wind chimes, decorations and a bunch of other seashell-use ideas. Invariably, however, I'll pause while writing, hold up my cheap plastic dry-erase marker and say, "Hey, if this were twenty years ago and I was using chalk on a chalkboard, I would recall that early chalk was made partially from ground up seashells."

Here I reminisce momentarily, wishing I could still teach in my early classrooms where chalkboards were the standard. There's nothing like chalk art, whether it be on a sidewalk or on a vertical board; it's such a nice medium for art. And then there's the classic fingernail screech. Years ago, I used that grating slice of sound to get the attention of a de-tuned class. I'm pretty sure the positive classroom discipline books wouldn't approve, but it worked. Ahh, chalkboards...

Sometimes students don't believe that early chalk was made of seashells. And later on, perhaps the next day of class, when I begin talking about tides and currents, the students who have never visited the ocean sometimes exhibit more disbelief, especially when I describe sea level rises and drops that exceed thirty feet in some places. I'm still trying to figure out how to communicate the nuances regarding major inland tidal rivers and tidal races. Maybe that's college level stuff.

Someone usually complains, "Mr. Doherty, this isn't science class, this is English! Why do we have to learn these words *neap* and *apposite* and *estuary*?"

I am very careful about teaching them the term *tidal bore*. I could respond that it's because they weren't paying attention in eighth grade geography, but I usually just say, "Every great writer has written about oceans and tides and currents. English is how we describe our world, so *anything* is fair game when teaching English!" But I perceive, that despite the complaints, students walk away from the lesson knowing just a little more about their world. Some of them will even look up the tide tables when they visit the coast next, and I can envision them with their parents, staring in awe at all the creatures in a tiny pool at low tide, curious and giddy as young children.

After using seashells for several years as a writing topic and reading passages from Rachel Carson again and again, I felt inspired to write some "ocean-y" words to one of my favorite traditional folk fiddle tune melodies, "Saint Anne's Reel." I titled it, "Where Sea Meets Land" by Marc Robertson. It goes as follows:

There's a beauty in walking on the ocean shore
Full of rocks and sand and so very much more,
Where the breakers that roll and wash in with the tides
Sing the primeval melodies of Earth.

It's no wonder that we always will return back there
Where the sea meets land in the salt-fresh air.
It's a place filled with mystery and filled with life,
Calling out to mankind's earliest dreams.

So, we walk once more along the deep blue sea
The source of every life and every memory,
Where the creatures who live are such a mystery
In this primeval harmony of Earth.

There's a mystery in sailing on the ocean waves
That goes back to humankind's earliest days,
When the world was such a brand new place to be
And great secrets always lay across the seas.

It was sailing on the ocean that transformed us then
To a wiser race with new science in our hands.
It is deep within the ocean that the secrets still rest,
And we now must set upon our greatest quest.

Yes we sail once more upon the deep blue sea
Where the tides ebb and flow before the salty breeze
Where the whales and the dolphins seem to swim so free
In their universe that flourishes so deep.

Near the end of our time writing about seashells, I usually perform Robertson's song for the class as an extra. Meanwhile, for starter songs, I work in Country Joe MacDonald's "Save the Whales" and a somewhat silly yet fun song "Where in the World are the Whales?" penned by a group named Northern Lights. And there are so many other songs, stories, poems—all inspired by rhythm and the tides.

Chapter 12: Yucca Braids and Desert

Rules, you gotta have 'em. Traditionally, classroom rules often read like this: "No Food or Drink" or "No Cellphones" or "No Bathroom Without Hall Pass." Math was one of my favorite subjects in school. I learned early on the difference between positives and negatives. I also learned that negatives tend to complicate equations more than positives. Same goes for rules. But what type of non-negative rule archetype would work for someone who loves the outdoors? "Keep Your Lifejacket Clipped" wouldn't transfer very well. So, I had to think about it for a while. After a year of muddling my way through the brushy thickets of public education classrooms, I felt like I needed a lifeline. I needed firm rules, but saying simply "no" just wouldn't work. I had already come up with the idea for the object-oriented writing topics when serendipity offered a solution. I was rummaging through an old box of mementos, looking for cool items to use as writing topics when I pulled out a four-foot piece of hand-braided yucca rope. I had created it many years earlier while taking an outdoor survival course. My bow and drill fire failed, but the ability to weave yucca braids stuck.

What a great writing topic! I thought to myself as I pulled out the braid and felt its unique texture. I tugged hard on the piece of rope. It held. I tugged harder. I couldn't break it. Wow, after all these years . . . then the yucca rope tugged back. *ROPE! It's an acronym!* R *is easy: Respect.* O *for On Time,* P *for Prepared, and* E . . . Here I paused for a time. *E, hmmm, energize? Naw. Excuse? Duh, that's opposite what I'm looking for. How about everyone participates? Not bad, but not quite what I'm looking for. Well,* E *is the only letter between* A *and* F *that we don't use for grades. Hey, it's all about earning grades, and an* A *stands for Excellence!!! Got it: Respect, On time, Prepared, Excellence. Class rules, ROPE.*

The key tool for rescue in the outdoors, rope, quickly became a key writing topic. It didn't take long for me to realize that the metaphor was as strong as the acronym. When day one for writing about rope begins, the call and response is particularly lively. I usually draw a huge, three-masted sailing ship on the whiteboard that takes up most of the board's twenty-foot length. On each mast, I outline four to five big square sails, and as we discuss *rope* as a class, I scrawl the metaphors into the blank space of the sails.

"When your stomach hurts, you might say that it's all . . ."

"It's all because I ate school lunch today." Everyone laughs.

"Funny, Jerry," I grin patiently, then start writhing my hands at my stomach. "Try again."

"Oh, it's tied up in knots!" he replies.

"Heather, you've just gotten a new job, but there's lots to learn. Somebody who has worked there for a while is assigned to do what with you?"

"Teach me how to do things?"

I hold up a piece of colorful climbing rope. "Use this."

Heather hesitates, but someone from the back of the room shouts out, "Show you the ropes!"

"Thanks, Jeremy, but you really don't look like Heather. Ok, Heather, try this one. Your mom or dad are really mad. They've had enough. They can't take one bit more. They are . . .

"At the end of their rope!"

"Right. Hey Jeremy, you seem to be pretty savvy with metaphors. Try this one. When somebody is being really critical of you, they just won't let up, you might say what?

"Cut me some slack!" Everyone looks at Jeremy in astonishment.

"Excellent, Jeremy." I hold up the rope piece, first taut, then slack, and explain the terms.

"Molly, what do you say when your friends convinced you to do something that you really didn't want to do? You say you got . . ."

"Got roped into it!" Now the class stares at Molly. *How do you know these things?* someone else asks.

"Let's go back to Heather's job. After she's been shown the ropes, it's time for her to work on her own. Now the boss is considering . . ."

"Cutting her loose!"

"Hey, you gals and guys are getting it! When teachers try to make connections, they look for a . . . *a tie-in.* And when someone is late, they say they . . . *got hung up.* A person who takes a big risk and is right on the edge is . . . *walking a tight line.* People who hate commitments always want relationships with . . . *no strings attached.*

Sometimes I end by filling in the last few sails while saying, "Ok, now as we begin our writing, let's *tie it all together.* And we'll have this brainstorm graphic *fully rigged* after we *tie up a few loose ends.*" At this point, I draw flags on top of the sailing masts, turn around, and say, "Let's write. I want to see your writing notebooks in *ship shape.*"

The yucca braid rope additionally holds extra significance, because it is a native plant, symbolic as the cactus for the arid West. On a good day, everyone takes advantage of the ten-minute quiet writing time as they weave the notes into a paragraph. I glance back at my somewhat rudimentary sketch of a sailing ship and think again of the last time I was on the water. Water in the arid West takes on a different magic than waters of oceans and coastal places. Even a simple morning or afternoon out on desert water gives me a great recharge. Near to home, I have a number of options: the Colorado and Green Rivers, the local mud puddles we call reservoirs, a few special mountain lakes, spring-fed calcium carbonate blue Bear Lake, and of course, The Great Salt Lake. Ahh, America's largest inland lake. Let me relate some thoughts revealed through a morning escape upon the Great Salt Lake. I penned these one Sunday evening after spending time on the lake. I titled the essay, "Changes Rippling Still Waters."

A unique form of vision is requisite when we attempt to truly understand Utah's Great Salt Lake. Where some see vast, empty expanses of lifeless water, others view a broad, painted landscape of reflections, as well as a hemispherically vital migratory ecosystem. Some turn away from a stench in the air, while others revel in salty freshness mixed with microbial phytoplankton, algae, and brine shrimp, all working in complex symbioses. And where some scoff at wastelands of deserted shores, others observe flora and fauna, moving in intricate balances, linked to the rise and fall of the largest hypersaline terminal lake in the western hemisphere.

The scale of the Great Salt Lake is best described by our senses as we depart from shore in ocean kayaks. My wife Deborah moves forward in front of me as I stop to photograph the flight of several Great Blue Herons, and when I look again, she is rapidly becoming a speck on a sea of water. The lake's seventy-five mile by thirty-five-mile breadth hides many horizons beneath the curvature of the earth. I cannot see land beyond Deb's kayak, and now she herself takes up only a tiny fraction of my view. It's time to catch up.

Beyond Deb's kayak, I see thousands of Eared Grebes that start as dots and meld into a smoke-like haze of life drifting at water level. When I stop and listen, I hear the subdued rushing of wings and webbed feet, of dips and resurfacings. The grebes are feeding on the brine flies and the brine shrimp. Mixed in with the grebes are seagulls, several varieties of ducks, and the occasional cormorant, sailing above the water. It's migration season, and literally dozens of species are apt to be visible on this September day.

Deb motions at a pair of Bald Eagles, and almost simultaneously I discern a flock of White Pelicans moving far in the distance. We've managed to enjoy an hour now without hearing the report of shotgun reverberating across the waters, but I know this serenity will not last. Although I accept hunting, I do not grasp killing. Many, many shooters are there just for the sport, just for the kill. Utah is one of the last states where most outdoorsmen haven't grasped the notion that one can also shoot wildlife with a camera.

I'm distracted from thoughts on arcane hunting practices when I notice a spit of land exposed that I've not seen before. The lake is now at its lowest level on record. Growing populations, water needs, and drought have wrought other changes. Yet I know that few people consider this lake in the context of Owens Lake, the Aral Sea, or Lake Urmia.

Shortsightedness regarding the Great Salt Lake stems from several factors, one being a dearth of research done on the lake and its greater ecosystem. Science largely overlooked this lake up until the late 1990s. We are learning now, but there is much to know. Why has the Great Salt Lake not been studied more? Some say it's because there aren't many terminal lakes, so they don't attract scientific attention. Others claim that salt lakes are uninteresting, limited in the numbers of species they harbor. And of course vast, shallow salt lakes seem to have little economic impact—money drives science.

But as I paddle forward, I can see the tiny plume of smoke coming from the magnesium plant twenty miles to the west. And I know that to my north, a 45,000-acre evaporation plant is producing six million tons of salt each year. Another company creates vast stores of fertilizer from the lake's brine shrimp. The lake supplies 1.3 billion dollars in economy to the state, and it provides 7,700 jobs. The lake is rich in life and minerals, and the impacts of harvesting are being felt before the science of the lake is fully understood.

I move alongside Deb and our paddles stroke side by side on glass. It's a perfectly calm morning. Reflected in the mirror of water are clouds floating above the blue lines of distant mountains. We are paddling through a sublime painting, vast and colorful, ever-changing.

"Did you hear the Grebes?" Deb asks.

"Yes, when I stopped to photograph you disappearing in the distance. It was remarkable."

"There must be thousands of them."

"Yep. And the eagles, thanks for the heads up."

We move with even strokes toward our destination: out there somewhere. Soon we'll stop, five or six miles from shore, and just float for a while, listening to the sounds, soaking up the silences. No other boats are out today. Few boats travel these waters. The salt is hard on motors, the shallow bottom difficult for keels. At this low, low level, "The World's Saltiest Sailors" of the Great Salt Lake Yacht Club must hope for rain and snow in the mountains—hope for the lake to rise again.

"I just poked for the bottom. It's only two feet deep here."

"Imagine a big windstorm and three-foot waves. Or rather, don't!" she smiles back at me.

We paddle on in silence for a time. "Sure hope this lake doesn't dry up in my lifetime."

"Those windstorms we've been having with this drought would have some pretty scary minerals to throw around in our air. Gives a new meaning to downwinders doesn't it?"

"Wow, that's another factor I hadn't thought about. I was still on the snow and Ski City USA wavelength."

Just last week the local news reported two stories in one newscast. The first was the Utah Travel Council vying for the name of Ski City USA, proclaiming as always that the Wasatch Mountains have the greatest snows on earth. The second reported the Bear River Water Conservancy's plans to divert enough water—220,000-acre-feet per year—to cause the lake to drop a foot or more. The irony? The greatest snow comes directly from evaporation of the warm lake lifting over the escarpment of the Wasatch Range. If the lake dries up . . . Ski City might become an ecological misnomer.

It's difficult to think about economy, jobs, and pressures as we paddle through our painting. I hear a second distant shotgun blast, which sharply focuses reality. I'm grateful for the Division of Wildlife Resources rangers. They attempt to keep the hunters and poachers away from our beloved Antelope Island State Park, the sanctuary from which we often launch our kayaks while the bison, antelope, and coyotes curiously watch us.

We've stopped paddling and are sliding smoothly forward, slowing. Deb has noticed a distant line of darker blue on the water's surface, maybe a mile off. It's the first sign of the breeze we expect to come from the North today. It's time to settle on the water for a time. Another flock of birds flies high overhead. They are not geese, but perhaps White Faced Ibis? Deb thinks they are swans and takes out her binoculars. Naturally, she is right.

I look back to Antelope Island, reflected perfectly on the lake's surface. Another group of cormorants moves over the water, flying inches above the surface. Beyond them I catch the graceful sweep of two Great Blue Herons, gliding with seeming effortlessness. They too seem to be riding a thin cushion of air just above the surface of the water.

I close my eyes and listen to the distant grebes, the even more distant California Gulls on Egg Island. The air is pure and sweet. It's only along the shores that one smells the chemistry of The Great Salt Lake. Once on the water, it's as fresh as ocean breezes. This is one more of our little secrets. With my eyes closed, I taste the salt on my lips and feel the slight grittiness of salt on my paddle. When we return today I must wade in and bob like a cork for a few minutes. One can stand straight upright in the water without stroking, without sinking. Although now it's difficult to find a place deep enough. My swim trunks can later stand by themselves after they dry if I forget to rinse them out.

The breeze has caught us, and tiny riffles appear around our kayaks. Without speaking, we lift our small sails and begin gliding homeward. The gifts of wildlife, solitude, and beauty rest easily in our minds. But how long can this place keep on giving in such a manner? We belong to the conservation organizations: Friends of the Great Salt Lake, Sierra Club, Utah Wilderness. We purchase a state parks pass each year. And yet it seems like we do so little amidst the pressures of industry, hunting, water, development and above all, climate change. And of course, we write. At least we can say, if the day dawns with malevolent dusts sweeping a dry lake bottom, at least we can say we did something, and we did it with passion.

By the time I've located my handouts for today's language lesson and readings, someone is already on a cell phone. Reminiscence over, time to get back to work.

"Hey Aaron," I say, breaking the writing silence which I know can't possibly last two minutes more, "Did you know that the Native Americans used to tie horses with yucca braids? That's how strong it is."

Aaron looks up from his cell phone, startled.

"Do you know why I don't use yucca braids to tie cell phones up?" I reach behind me for an item on the nearby bookshelf. "It's because *duct tape* has a better sound when it's used!" I proceed to tape Aaron's phone to the desk, and we move on to our language lesson for the day.

Chapter 13: Mystery and Superstition

"Dad and I went out shooting birds this weekend!" spouts second grader Billy as he struts into the classroom.

"Wow," answers second-grade teacher, Mr. Roy. "Did the birds shoot back?"

Little Billy stops short, wrinkles his brow, and stammers, "Uh, I dunno."

"Hang your coat up, Billy. You've still got ten minutes before the bell," says Mr. Roy. Then he turns back to me. "Ok, Mark, what does my student teacher have ready for today?"

Brilliant, simple, effective. My long-time friend Phil Roy who offered to mentor my student teaching in his second grade-classroom has just shown me how humor and wit can diffuse a bomb. I can see Billy's head from where he's plunked himself in his desk. He isn't moving, but I'll bet his mind is. I'll bet he's seeing a monstrous meadowlark holding a double-barrel shotgun saying, "Ok Kid, you won the first round. Now it's my turn! Can you RUN?"

It's the imagination that makes young children so much fun to teach. Phil knew this, Robert Fulghum knew this, and I came to know this as well. I never got to teach my own elementary classroom full of impressionable young minds, other than that brief substitute stint with sixth graders just before landing hard in high school. But the lessons in creativity I learned from eight weeks with Phil lasted for an entire career. And they were lessons that the young students taught me, like Sarah who wrote her first poem under my tutelage:

I remember,
It was the night
That the clouds
Were hands
Taking the moon.

There were many more, but for some reason, that one stuck. Years later I would recite those lines when discussing imagery with creative writing students. More importantly, during all the years of teaching high school students, I returned time and again to imagination-stirring ideas and activities, always with the hope of reawakening the child within each older student.

One year I was struggling to articulate the power of literary allusion to my advanced placement seniors. Still teaching small classes in rural Utah, I had time to experiment; furthermore, I had an administration that trusted my credentials and let me become a true teacher. So I decided to try an experiment with my seniors. Halloween was approaching. After completing our SLC activity for the day (spontaneous literary criticism), I scrawled the thirteen-letter word *superstitions* vertically on the chalkboard.

"Write me an acrostic poem for *superstitions*. Use an allusion to a well know author. Winner gets a black sock full of candy corns! You have forty minutes and can use any book in the room. Go." This was during the pre-cell phone, pre-laptop, early pc era when quality classrooms hosted lots and lots of books of all kinds. I settled in to grade their recent literary criticism essays and let them go.

The poems were amazing. Students alluded to authors ranging from Hawthorne to Twain, Poe to Whitman, and even Wollstonecraft to Fuller. Of course, when I posted the poems on the door with some seasonal decorations, most readers thought them weird, strange, and didn't understand some of the lines. But that didn't matter. *I* knew the allusions. *They* knew the allusions. And for the rest of the year, literary allusions in text were caught like pop fly balls in a softball game.

Where are those poems now? They were indeed great poems. Someday, we'll see one of them in our world of poetry and I'll say, "Hey, I knew that person once!" Meanwhile, I've adapted the activity in a number of ways. I now call this activity "Slam with a Slant." The most recent iteration of the lesson employs an acrostic poem of my own:

> ***S***tudents, you will now
> ***U***ndertake a challenging
> ***P***roject.
> ***E***veryone will write *acrostic* poems
> ***R***elating somehow to
> ***S***uperstition as a
> ***T***heme or concept, and all done
> ***I***n a time frame of
> ***T***hirteen minutes.
> ***I*** will then select thirteen writers
> ***O***f these poems that will
> ***N***ext, take the podium up front and
> ***S***lam-recite their poem to the class!

There is a crossover between childhood and adulthood that takes place with activities like this. It's fun to participate in. But sometimes this level of creativity threatens those who are not creative or who are not comfortable with the type of free-thinking that springs from it.

Here's an example from my days in rural Utah teaching at a small school. Every year we hosted a hide-and-seek contest using what we called a *Spirit Stick*. Every day of Homecoming Week would begin with the search for the stick. The class (as in sophomore, junior, senior) who found the stick the most times was the acclaimed winner and most filled with homecoming spirit that year. Not long after being hired, I was asked to hide the spirit stick and write the hints. Our homecoming director asked me to make them *hard* hints because kids were finding the spirit stick too easily and the game didn't last long enough. I went to work. Every hour between morning classes a new hint would be announced. I made them hard, and the students rose to the occasion surprising all of us. By hint three, someone always figured out the puzzle and found the stick. Rarely did they find it on hint two, almost never on hint one. I also attempted to get some cross-curricular applications into the hints. The writing of the hints and the game that ensued was so memorable that I still have all the old hints. Here are a few examples including the preliminary game rules:

2002 Spirit Stick Hiding Places & Hints

Students remember, nothing needs to be altered, removed, or taken apart in order to find the Spirit Stick. The Spirit Stick will not be in any classroom, nor will it be in the library, auditorium, shop, gymnasiums, football field area, bathrooms, or faculty areas! The boundaries are the streets surrounding the school and the creek. If you find the stick on the way to class, show it to your teacher immediately as the bell rings. If you are out of class looking for the Spirit Stick, your class will be disqualified from that day's Spirit Stick Competition and points will be awarded to the other classes.

Now here's hint number one for Monday. Good Luck Hunters!!

Monday's Location: base of west outdoor stairs

(Hint 1)
A place for safe ascension
Maybe M.C. Escher's style,
Or Led Zeppelin's song intention
When pointed towards the sky.

(Hint 2)
Upon the leeward side
Of where the east wind blows,
Spirit will abide
Where summers remnants go.

(Hint 3)
Sidewalks slice green grass,
As summer's last winds blow,
And steps collect the last,
That's where your Spirit goes.

Tuesday's Location: window sill above office

(Hint 1)
Silicates have made me
Yet diaphanous am I,
Watching over incumbency
Is where Spirit spies.

(Hint 2)
Kissinger and Adams
And even Jefferson,
All held this position,

Just like old Hamilton.

(Hint 3)
High above the talking
I can see it all,
You can see me watching
When answering your call.

Wednesday's location: south hall fire extinguisher

(Hint 1)
Enthused, inspired, or smitten,
Impassioned, stirred, aroused,
A metaphor to catch these all
Is a spirited hideout.

(Hint 2)
It's very elemental,
It feeds from number eight,
But number six is what it eats,
If Spirit stays too late.

(Hint 3)
Conflagrations cease,
Where your spirit hides,
Sweet tooth if you please,
Spirit is close by.

Thursday's Location: old motor beside shop

(Hint 1)
The horses race in stampedes fast,
Refined history makes them roar,
Sparked by explosions their heads blast,
Spirit lingers where they run no more.

(Hint 2)
The Beach Boys sang about it in 409,
And it was a verse in Born to be Wild,
But this one sits silent in rain and snow,
Yet Spirit remembers when it used to go.

(Hint 3)
A block of wood,
A block of town,
A block of metal,
Is where Spirit's found.

For the last day, which was Friday morning, I asked the math teacher to post a math problem revealing the number of a locker under which the spirit stick was taped. We had to be sure that the spirit stick was found on the first hint because the homecoming assembly took place in the morning after second-hour classes.

But as I mentioned earlier, sometimes it seemed like some people were envious, even superstitious of creativity. One fellow faculty member said to his students about my writing of the spirit stick hints, "Oh, he just sits around at night smoking pot and dreaming up ideas." Ouch. That one hurt. As a dedicated public educator, a devout bicycle commuter and outdoorsman, endorphins and a little bit of completely legal alcohol made up the entirety of *my* drug use. I wouldn't even ask for painkillers beyond Motrin from dentists and doctors. When I first heard that he'd said this, I didn't believe it. I thought students were making it up. Then I heard it from two other students and one fellow faculty member. I was surprised because he was a great teacher whom I respected. It seemed that he had a chip on his shoulder. I'm guessing it had something to do with his cultural roots being planted in Utah, whereas my uprooted transplant originated in Boulder, Colorado.

Now that I think about it from this vantage point in the future, if endorphins can be considered a drug, maybe creativity can be thought of as an inebriant as well. In that case, I'm addicted—have been for years, and there's no cure! I would love to hear that someone said, "Oh, he just sits around doing *creativity* all night. Guilty and glad!

Chapter 14: A Menagerie of Objects

By the end of each teaching year, the top of a low bookshelf and a medium-sized bulletin board above it becomes a sort of writing topic shrine, hosting a menagerie of objects that we wrote about during the year. The long crane feather rises above it all nearly touching the ceiling, and the polished round slice of firewood featuring its tree-rings stands center stage. The rest of the objects gather around the shelf top and the bulletin board like a crowd of diverse concert-goers, each striking its own unique pose. I probably don't do a good enough job reminding students to look back and reflect on all we've discussed, but I know they get it, even if it's on an intuitive and unseen level. For me, it is a shrine of a different nature; maybe I should say it's a shrine mostly related to nature. Even items such as an old antique iron lead to discussions of metals and resources and the Great Lakes and great shipping disaster tales like Gordon Lightfoot's song "The Wreck of the Edmund Fitzgerald." That particular starter song takes a bit of work to keep fully memorized! Another topic, an old transistor radio opens up discussions of Morse Code, radio waves, ionosphere, sun spots, and even the Northern Lights.

There is always a mix of objects. Some come strictly from nature, while others are man-made. The natural world is easy to relate to with most of the objects though, such as a 1946 *Audubon Field Guide to Eastern Land Birds* with full-color plates, all done by hand. When relating to another object, an old Huck Finn style leather hat, we can discuss how something as simple as clothing styles can and has driven animal species such as the flamingo and the beaver and the otter to near extinction—great material for a broader critical essay on consumerism and business ethics.

Then it's time to pull out the deer antlers, some fishing gear, a few wreaths made from willows, and even an old forest service trail marker sign. We get to discuss hunting ethics, the evolution of catch-and-release fishing, the folklore of the wreath, the essential nature of willows in Western ecosystems, and what trails on our public lands are all about—even when locals do not want them. An old pair of canvas Mukluks, inexpensive substitutes for sealskin boots, lately make wonderful discussion regarding climate change. They are also so funky that kids want to dance around the room in them while someone takes a Facebook shot. For a while, when the movie *Balto* was popular, I could also connect the boots to the names of the polar bears Muck and Luck. And when teaching in rural Utah, where some students came from farming and ranching families, I used to take out an old hand-braided bullwhip. Students loved to make it pop—loud as a small rifle; administrators tolerated the antics. The connotations of a whip in the city, however, have caused me to keep the bullwhip in the box. But its sure opened discussions of public lands grazing, horse-whispering, and Western traditions. And speaking of traditions, the old wooden hand plane always worked well for discussing craftsmanship and things made by hand from natural resources such as trees versus petroleum products and overseas outsourcing. Ah, trees, I almost forgot the original Moab, Utah artist Serena Supplee's watercolor painting of a juniper tree in winter entitled *Einstein's Hair on Purple Trunk*. Not only could I talk about knowing the artist personally, but we also discussed what it takes to professionally mat and frame a painting, to name a painting, to own an original.

Once indoctrinated into the idea that objects of all sorts can make great discussion and writing topics, students often offer to bring me objects they would like to see me use.

"Hey, Mr. Doherty," a student asks me after class, "Can I bring in the next writing topic?"

"What did you have in mind, Waynee?"

"It's a hand-made Navajo saddle blanket! My dad got it when he went to Albuquerque a few years back."

"That does sound interesting. I'd love to see it, but I have to admit that I have too many objects already planned and set for writing topics. You know, I actually have to *think* about them and plan them out a bit. You'd have to leave the saddle blanket with me, and by next year I'd have something ready."

Wayne looks a bit crestfallen. "But bring it in and let me see it. And you know what Wayne, if you want to take what we do with other topics and create a series of lessons on your own about your saddle blanket, well, I'll count your work for that essay you missed."

Wayne leaves, satisfied. I'm relieved. Once again I've found a way to defer an offer for more stuff to write about. I wish I could use all their ideas. In fact, just the other day, while showing a student how much junk was in the writing topic boxes, stuff that will never get used, I came across a Ziploc bag with a few chunks of glass, purple glass. And yet another story popped into my head. I found these particular pieces while on a weekend getaway backpacking trip in the desert. It was yet another trip away from school meant to recharge me for more school. And what a great writing topic purple glass would make. . .

Finding Purple Glass

History Jewels they might be called. Trash turned treasure. They are, simply, chunks, pieces, slivers, and on rare occasions complete articles of glass. But they have been turned from clear or green glass into pale lavender or dark purple by time and the sun. Lying forgotten in the ruins of cabins, ghost towns, mining mills, they wait like arrowheads for the delighted explorer to pick them up and marvel at them. Finding purple glass provides glee, wonder, and truly a glimpse into history.

During the glass producing eras of the late 1800's, glassmakers worked with numerous formulas to create glass. Pre-1880 glass was made with iron, lead or selenium. With time and sun exposure, iron turned the glass aqua, lead to gray, and selenium to yellow. Early glass always carried a tint from one or more of these elements. The public was worried about the tint tainting preserved foods; consequently, the glass companies concocted a new potion: clarified glass with manganese. Manganese is the magic ingredient in old glass. When left for months or even years in the sun to absorb ultraviolet rays, the manganese turns the glass into myriad shades of translucent purple. Antique shops throughout the states still specialize in these translucent treasures. After all, any glass manufactured that was old enough can be set out into the sun, away from little boy's stone throws, and left long enough, will turn purple. By 1914, however, WW I cut off the supply of German manganese to the U.S glass manufacturers. Soon they created newer recipes, and the purple glass supply was destined to become both antique and finite. Of course, modern glassmakers sometimes replicate purple glass, but without the bubbles, imperfections, straw marks, and unique styles, the ruse is easy to detect. Others try to use germicidal UV lamps on modern glass to purple it. A good collector will know the difference.

Finding purple glass beyond the scope of the antique store is something special. Yet, like arrowheads and pot shards, they are now becoming rarer. Nature has totally reclaimed much of their provinces, and treasure hunters have pocketed the bottles, broken or whole, for decades. Of course, the glass and the arrowheads and even the ancient pottery still exist on mantles, in drawers, in glass picture display cases throughout the country. Many artifacts are preserved long beyond their natural outdoor life due to the habits of collectors.

Picking up and pocketing purple glass seems for some reason less of an ethical issue than picking up an arrowhead or pottery shard. Why is this? Does it have to do with age? Arrowheads might be 600 or more years old, purple glass a mere 50 to 100. Arrowheads came from often mysterious cultures of which we know little history, or from cultures from which we failed to study history before stealing their cultures and land. Purple glass comes from mining towns turned ghost towns, old homesteads, trash heaps, and even cowboy camps. For a time, early telephone and telegraph wires were held on posts by glass insulators. Baking in the sun, they turned a beautiful dark purple. As a youngster, one of my favorite activities was to climb telephone poles and unwire purple insulators then screw a newer clear or green glass insulator back onto the threaded post and rewire the line. I was aware, growing up on an eight-party phone line, that some of those old lines were still in use! We always had someone keep watch, knowing that if caught, a fierce Ma Bell serviceman might pluck us from the pole and haul us off to his cave. Worse yet, he might call the local sheriff and our parents. Sometimes I felt guilty "stealing" purple glass that way—that was until I witnessed some other rural kids shooting insulators with their pellet guns and bb guns. What a waste of beautiful glass. One of my first lessons in levels of lawbreaking. I figured my karma was set, I later was to become a high school debate coach—lots of discussion regarding levels of crime. Perhaps some of the rifle-toting kids are now working in manual labor or juvenile detention centers. I still think my crime was relatively crimeless. I felt I was smuggling glass, they were destroying property.

Purple glass is, to some, not much of a mystery—manufactured in a factory around the turn of the century, hauled across the country in wagon, by mule, and later by steam locomotive.

It was probably used by. . . hold on a minute. Why is purple glass not much of a mystery? When I find a piece of it, my mind races through the history of America, the settling of the West, the mining boom and bust eras, the railroads, the telegraph. I wonder if the piece of jar or bottle I now hold in my hand once carried medicine, alcohol, food. I wonder if a cowboy or miner drank whiskey from it to ward off a bitter chilling storm. I wonder if a homestead wife used it a hundred times to preserve food before somehow it was lost and broken. I wonder why only some of the insulators on the old telephone poles were purple, the rest green or clear. I simply wonder, sometimes even more than when I find an arrowhead.

I find it almost as difficult to leave a piece of purple glass lying on the ground for others to see as it is to leave an arrowhead behind. When I was a youngster trading insulators, I sold all my purple insulators to the local antique shop for ice cream money. Today I admit to having scattered pieces about my garden, both of glass and arrowheads, gleaned from non-restricted areas. Too bad I didn't keep some of those fully intact purple insulators. But more often than not I have left most of my finds behind for others to see. My mind, however, goes wild every time I pick a piece up and hold it in my hands. Even when I gather up my garden pieces, I dream a little about an era in our country, a window of time, that was truly remarkable. Purple glass is indeed something worthy of note, from the whole intact museum or antique store piece to the shard found in a ghost town foundation. It is worth noting, it is worth scrutinizing, and it is always worth dreaming about. Part of the true American dream for me is being able to go out on public lands, search the remnants of forgotten peoples, and pick up fragments of purple glass and other relics from other times from perhaps that same American dream.

When I decide to add purple glass to the growing list of writing topics, I'm going to need a visit to one of those antique shops. A completely unbroken jar or an insulator would really be neat to show the kids. And the collection just keeps growing. Soon I'll need a fourth box to hold all those writing topics. When I retire, they'll make for a really wild garage sale.

Chapter 15: The Joy of Writing Purposeful Poetry

"Oh no!" I exclaimed. "The *first* poem in my *first* book has a spelling error!" I placed my little hand-made poetry book on the dinner table in front of my parents and pointed at the carefully typewritten pages, tears streaming down my face. I was ten years old and in sixth grade.

"Which word, Mark, do you think is wrong?" asked my mother.

"It's this one," I pointed. "Cactuses."

"What is it supposed to be?" asked Dad.

"It's *Cacti!*" I sniffed. "I just saw it in our book on desert flowers. I can't turn in a book for my project with a *mistake* on the first page! And it's wrong in the contents too."

Dad rose from the dining room table and walked into the living room, returned with a copy of *Webster's New World Dictionary*. "Now let's see, hmm, *cacomistle, cacophony. . . ah, cactus."* Then he paused, set the dictionary in front of me and waited for me to wipe the tears from my eyes. "Read the entry, Mark."

"See, it says *cacti* as plu . . . oh. It says, *or cactuses!* They are *both* right!"

Dad picked up my book and gently closed the soft cardboard cover over the lovingly manual typewriter produced pages and handed it to me. "Even if you had misspelled a word, it would still be a wonderful poetry book."

More than forty years pass, and the old Smith-Corona manual typewriter becomes an antique. Yet I still stress out about typos in my lesson handouts, and I still write poems. Once a week, or once every two weeks when teaching a crazy block schedule, I pen a new poem for my students' writing topic. Often, I write the poem right in front of them as I explain my simple rules for writing traditional poetry: 1) Use one margin and don't center your lines. 2) Capitalize the first letter of each line. 3) Use punctuation! and 4) Title your poem. I know that I could use the same example poem year after year, but the truth of the matter is that writing poetry is *fun.* It is *rewarding.* It offers a challenge every time. And so today I'm standing in front of the chalkboard staring over at the pair of antlers on the writing topic desk. I need an example poem for my students, one that is just the right mix of simple and complex, something that has a theme or lesson in it, and maybe including a few new words for them. I write,

Antler Lore—Vanishing Buck

Residing in the forest deep,
The Great Stag stands guard—
His majestic rack held high
As a symbol of age, stature, and wisdom.

But he only appears from the ethereal mists
Within the crosshair sight of ill-intended hunters
Whose selfishness triggers the magic
Of vanishing mirages, mythical beasts.
Only the empty shell remains,
Testimony to an out-of-season shot
From the darker side of man.

"I have nothing against hunters," I tell my students, "but I abhor poachers."

Several of boys in my rural Utah classroom nod in approval. They come from ranching and hunting families and often show me pictures of their trophies.

"But I will tell you all again, even though I'm an omnivore, I only hunt with a camera; that's just my personal style and choice. Most of the authors from early American conservation movements were hunters, Leopold, Thoreau, even Roosevelt. Although Thoreau did say that if humanity seeks a higher evolutionary plane they will leave off eating meat." I pause. "Just wanted to throw out a carrot to the vegetarians in the crowd." Nobody gets it. I move on. "Ok, ten minutes to craft a poem, then it's on to the second half of Faulkner's *The Bear*. We need to finish the reading today."

A week later, the class is using seashells as a writing topic. I need a poem that uses a few new words like *ebb* and *flood.* I need to portray the feeling of waves, the power of the sea. I wonder if I can also appeal to my young students' sense of the ups and downs of life as a teenager. Hmm. Let's try this one:

Washed Ashore

I comb the beach at daybreak
For treasures it may hold,
Knowing that the waves last night
Were strong and high and bold.

The anger of the ocean,
The anger in my mind,
Seemed to flood together
In waves of a like kind.

But now the storm's abated,
Waves ebbed before the dawn,
And I find washed ashore
A hope to carry on.

"We wrote about the tides in yesterday's lesson. Can you find a way to include the concept of tides, oceans, moons into a poem? Can you imagine finding a seashell washed ashore? Maybe something else washed ashore? Time to write."

And then there are the many poems I've crafted as examples for the topic of the old hunk of firewood and the trees it represents. This year I'm using the tree topic at the same time I'm teaching Patrick Henry and Thomas Paine, Benjamin Franklin and Thomas Jefferson. I've added an old bicentennial poster produced by the National Forest Service entitled, "America's History is in Her Trees," which features a 200-year-old spruce tree section showing the concentric growth rings. Key historical events are printed in boxes around the edges of the poster with arrows pointing to the tree ring that coincides with the year, such as the pith year, 1776, signing of the Declaration of Independence, Transcontinental Railroad, 1869, Founding of the National Forest Service, 1876, Orville and Wilbur Wright's Flight, 1903 and a dozen other significant American historical events. The major wars are also listed, such as the Civil War, WW I, and WW II. Gazing at the poster, I ruminate over the idea, then scrawl this poem on the chalkboard:

America the Evergreen

A small seed was once watered
With liberty, freedom, justice—
And grew, earning its place
In the forest of history.

Its constitution strengthened,
Yet it was challenged while still a sapling
By gales of a civil revolution,
And hurricanes of world war.

Now an aging monarch,
Its limbs branch far into the world around it.
But what genus begets its origin?

Is it the fir, the spruce, or the bristlecone pine?
Will it withstand the storms of time?

A year later, however, I couldn't find my tattered folder crammed full of previous writing topic poems, and I couldn't remember the previous year's poem for trees. So, I wrote a new one, and the next year, another new poem. Now I have a forest of tree poems written as writing topic examples. It seems like there should also be a metaphor for teachers and the seeds of knowledge in there somewhere, but for now, I only see the nearby tree poems, like these:

I'm The Old Bristlecone

I stand on the mountain,
High up and alone,
Bent, ancient, and twisted;
I'm the old Bristlecone.

When Odysseus sailed
On his quest from his shore,
Or when chariots clashed
In Caesar's great war,

I was here on the mountain
With limbs reaching high,
And I'd already seen
A thousand years pass by.

Now I'm four thousand,
And what is in store?
Someday, like all things,
I'll stand here no more.

Bristlecone Fine

Imagine a tree
Living high and alone,
Twisted with age,
Gnarled by storm,
Ancient yet growing—
It's the old Bristlecone.
Four thousand years

It has stood thriving strong;
There is little on earth
That has survived so long.
August and imposing,
Worthy of poems
Worthy of song
Bristlecone pine
So old, yet so fine.

Wisdom

Standing tall in the great forest,
The mighty spruce catches
Messages drifting by
Which were written in the wind.
Sighing with understanding,
The tree lifts limbs towards
The knowing stars as it becomes
Silhouetted by sunset.
This gentle giant of the woods sees and hears
Much great wisdom in the passing years.

Violin

Cut from
A long dead
And carefully cured
Ancient spruce tree,
The wood was
Expertly carved,

Shaped, molded,
Tuned, and fitted
By the master craftsman.
The lacquer applied,
Strings taut and ready,
It was finally delivered
From the womb of creativity
By the sensitive hands
Of the concert musician.

Tall Wise Trees

Knowledge is a seed
Planted in the fertile soils
And loamy earthen darkness
Of the mind.
With nourishment and water,
It grows, leaves, and blossoms—
As the seasons pass.
And if the tree is nourished,
Protected from storms
That can cut its life
Into truncated ruin,
The tree will rise above
The great forest
And stand—a monument
To learning.

Seedling Silence

When you see my greenery,
My blossoms, cones, or fruits
As they flourish amidst
The sunshine of our acquaintance,
Just remember that beneath
There's so much more.
Few can ever know
How deep roots run.
Friendship begins
When you plant seeds,
And start to know
My deepest needs.

Beyond the forest of tree poems and ideas, however, lies a veritable wilderness of other poems—all composed for the writing topics that change from week to week, year to year.

When I take a trip back down the dusty pathways of my youth and search the labyrinthine shelves of my memory, I sometimes can recall steps to my evolution as a poet and writer. One memory from tenth grade English class comes to mind. Our class was spending the hour in the library, and our teacher asked us all to compose ten-minute poems, which were to be shared with the class as oral readings. An easy task for me. I loved poetry, and so I cranked out a poem about mustaches. It was inspired by some miscreant's artwork on the faces of a magazine cover in the magazine rack next to my table. Evidently the librarian had not yet noticed it, otherwise, the magazine would have been pulled. My number to read aloud came up early, and so I proudly produced my poem, then sat down.

Not more than five students later, a girl named Julie was called to read her poem. I didn't really know Julie, other than knowing that she wore glasses and was somewhat of a silent bookworm type. She read her poem, which was about trees, or rather it was about one particular tree. But it was also a poem about creativity and ideas. She created an extended metaphor starting with seeds of creation, moving through growth, blossoms, fruition—and ending with the deep roots of human experience. The poem also had rhyme, rhythm, alliteration, and assonance. Of course, I didn't yet know what rhythm really meant, let alone assonance and alliteration, but I sensed them as she read. Two things I did know however were one, I was jealous. Everyone in the library was blown away. You could tell by the second of complete silence just prior to the applause. The second thing I knew was that I was going to write poems until I could write one as good as hers. Yes, I'm still writing poems. I know now that I have penned poems as thoughtful as Julia's, but just like a first kiss or a first date, I'll always remember her poem from English class.

And now it's my own English class, and poetry is still a major force in my teaching paradigm. If the fat-as-a-fist "What Do I Do With This?" folder gets forgotten in the back of my file, it's probably because there is an equally fat file stuffed in the cabinet that lives a much more active life. It's the folder crammed full of poems I've penned for teaching, and only now am I attempting to cull through them and type them into a document. As I type them, each and every poem reminds me of a specific week from "Daily Writing," and later named "Weekly Writing" due to block schedule teaching, which extended five daily writings into two weeks of writings—I only saw each class every other day. The same objects, year by year, landed on the desk or the table or the counter or the bulletin board, but every year I felt compelled to write new poems, or perhaps revise poems from previous years. Why did I feel the need to write new poems? Why revise old poems? I mean, if a lesson works well, and if the text of the lesson is good, why change it? Perhaps the answer lies in the reality of teaching the same subject, the same grade levels, the same curriculum year after year. Some teachers just can't stand it. They hate the repetition. They hate the routine. It becomes boring. And I see their argument. For certain, there is a significant amount of routine that goes into teaching. But then I consider my starter songs, and I consider the songwriters and singers who have made these poems classics of American culture. What made poets like Gordon Lightfoot, or John Denver, or Joni Mitchell, or Kate Wolf, or Marc Robertson able to perform the same songs year after year, concert after concert? The answer to this is complex, multifaceted, unique to each artist; however, a few factors might explain the basics. For one, the audience is constantly changing. Secondly, a good poem is worth reading and rereading countless times, because at every different stage and time of life it speaks differently to the reader (and to the author, I might add). And finally, there is a type of meditation that happens in poetry and song, not unlike prayer, that is always worthy of remembering and repeating. So there we have it; in education, the same basic principles apply. For me as a poet, I always felt that my poems were works in progress, so naturally, from year to year, I liked to improve them. The same goes for my lessons. Whoever dreamed that teaching a lesson once would yield teaching perfection? Whoever thought that even five times would make a lesson perfect? No, it takes years of teaching the same lesson to hone it, to carve off the unnecessary parts and polish the essential, to focus on the essence, to create the impact. Even when I taught six classes each day of the same subject, the same lesson, I never tired of the performance and of the desire to make it better. By the sixth lesson, I usually felt that things were working pretty well. But six tries were all I got because it was time to move on to the next day, the next lesson, the next subject, the next unit, the next curricular objective. And I knew it would be a year, at least, before I got to return to the lesson of the day, and often the poem of the day. It would be a year before I got to run that river again, and by then, many of the rapids and the eddies would change.

The components of lessons, and particularly of the elements of poetry writing that I employ every year, are subject to change. Sometimes that change is a spur-of-the-moment change, and I scrawl or print a copy of the changed or revised poem and stuff it in the folder, hoping to remember to use the new idea for the next year. And indeed, quite often, I rummage through the folder of poems looking for a former idea I want to resurrect. But that's also a dangerous and distracting proposition, for inevitably I come across a dozen other poems with new ideas that I also hope to employ, all unrelated to the topic or current need at hand, and I become lost in a storm of possibilities. I remember losing a full fifteen minutes of prep time to reminiscence one day when I pulled a poem from the folder that I distinctly remembered as one of my old "chalkboard poems" from teaching in rural schools. Flashback! Doing that *creativity* drug again!

During the 1990's, my classrooms hosted classic chalkboards, and I realize now that the medium of a chalkboard, chalk, and eraser actually contributed to my evolution as a poet. The ease of erasing words or lines, sometimes even entire stanzas of a poem, became wonderfully liberating when I chalked out the example poems for writing topics. There is something larger than paper that happens when a poem goes up in poster size words on the board; there is a magic to the swipe of the eraser and the click-hiss strokes of new words and lines. It feels a little bit like being a Picasso of poetry. Revising poems on paper is enjoyable. Revising poems on a computer is easy. Revising poems on a chalkboard is exhilarating. I maintain that some of the revision techniques I now employ with poems evolved while working on that great expanse of slate. I still revise on the board, but it's a whiteboard with dry-erase markers. It works, but the sound and the smell and the feel are all missing, and when the plastic pen is out of ink, it gets thrown away. I miss the brand-new three-inch piece of white or yellow chalk. I miss the dime-sized nubbin that has one more poem in it. I miss the tradition of the chalkboard. But when I sift through the folder of poems, I always find a few that I distinctly recall being written on those great slate pages. Someday I'll get another chalkboard, just for poetry. Maybe I'll design a poetry slam technique whereby poets pen their words in chalk before the audience. Imagine writing a word, then erasing it, then writing a synonym . . . you get the idea.

Meanwhile, we're writing about transistor radios next week, and I have about twenty poems penned to the title, "I Heard it on the Radio." It's time to try for twenty-one.

Chapter 16: Teaching Creative Writing

"*Finis Originae Pendet,*" I say, pointing to a small poster in front of the room. "What does this mean?"

Silence.

"Ok, let's work it out. *Finis* looks like what word?"

"Finish," states Robin.

"Good. Now give me some synonyms for *finish.*"

"Line!" exclaims Carl. "Finish line!"

I look at Carl with an indulgent smile. "Carl, I asked for synonyms, not *sillynyms.*" Everyone laughs. Soon students come up with *completion, conclusion, ending, close, and stop.*

"Good. Now tell me what the Latin *originae* reminds you of. We establish *originate,* and shortly synonyms such as *start, begin, open, commence,* and *introduce.*

"Now for the hard one. I'll help you out to begin with. Look at Sara's necklace. What is one name you can give to the pretty blue stone she has around her neck?" It doesn't take long to establish *pendent*, but it takes a little more time to get the word *depend* from them.

"The end depends upon the beginning," I state simply. And it's time to start a new class, or a new year, or a new lesson . . .

It's day one in Creative Writing Class. I have a class size that seems now like a dream: seventeen students. Last spring, I convinced our principal of our 450-student rural school that this would be a useful elective, and I've promised to produce an informal literary magazine as well: Here we go.

The bell finishes its interminable ringing, and I say, "Welcome to Creative Writing. I believe that every one of you is a creative writer. I believe you are all born with it. This class is about simply opening the right doors of your minds and exploring what's inside."

Students look a bit puzzled. So, I continue, "All right, If I believe you are already creative writers, then how do you think you can earn an A in this class?"

A hand shoots up. "By how much you write?"

"Nope, try again."

Another hand. "Homework?"

"Nope, homework's up to you. Do it, or don't. It won't make a grade difference."

A pause ensues, then a third hand. "Attendance?"

"Ah, now you are warm, getting close, smelling the smoke from the campfire. But you're not quite there warming your hands yet. What's that old cliché, *if at first, you don't succeed . . .?"*

"Try, try again!" comes a response.

I clap my hand sharply. "Got it. All you have to do is try, make an effort, attempt, endeavor, aim, venture, go for it, take the leap, dive in, test the waters. You just have to try."

I pause before a somewhat bemused class. Many of these students have taken my English class already, or they are in English this year. I can see them wondering, *What's he up to?* What they don't know is that I'm taking a completely new approach. There is no curriculum, thank God, there is only creativity and my own experience. There is also a pretty good book I once read on creative writing, way back in the 1970's at Colorado University in a creative writing class. Of course, it's out of print, and my investigations into the whereabouts of the author or publisher in the late 1990's yields nothing. So, I make a class set of the book in the copy center and bind it myself with those little plastic rings, and we're off.

"We have one textbook for this class," I continue on day one, "And that is this book, *Sweet Agony* by Gene R. Olson. I wanted to order it for the class, but it's out of print now, and it's not available anywhere, so I photocopied a class set. But it's only 118 pages long."

I distribute the books, which have all been carefully numbered. Then I open up my original copy. "Let's get started." I hold up my original copy with the distinctive orange tan and black cover hosting a smattering of typewriter letters, open the front cover and say, "Notice the price. $2.75 Used. Now that's what I call an affordable textbook!" A few of my seniors who are also enrolled in English 1010 shake their heads and smile. They just purchased their $65 texts for *that* writing class. I instruct students, "Open your books to chapter one." I start reading:

"A Great Place to Begin

You sit there, see, staring at that stark white piece of paper . . .

Which wouldn't be so bad except that . . . IT STARES BACK.

What's worse, it whines and wheedles and whinnies: "I want words. Give me words. Lots of words. Lovely Words. Immortal words. *Don't leave me blank!*"

There, in a quivering capsule, is the writer's problem.

And that's what this book is about.

(Gee. Maybe it should be a bigger book.)"

(Gene R. Olson)

I stop, look for a smile or two. "Like his tone? He's a comedian, isn't he?" I turn around and pick up a stack of plain white copy paper. "So am I. Here's your first blank page! Write me a poem. Title it *The Blank Page*. You have fifteen minutes. I'll write one with you. Go!

At the end of fifteen minutes, we all read our poems out loud to pencil tapping applause. Nobody gets a pass on reading their poem, even if it's just one line long—even if it's simply an eye sketched in the middle of the page. (Yes, that did happen, so I exacted a quick oral poem out of the kid while he held up the eye drawing for all to see).

Like the first drops of a summer shower, the words hit our senses and the wonderful storm of creativity let loose. Within a week of class, pages full of words were flooding over my desk and spilling into the *I can't get it all read* gutter. And that's another secret to teaching writing. Copious amounts of writing must be done in order for selective gems of writing to happen. My strategy has always been to be honest with students. I tell them that sometimes I read everything they write, but most often I pick randomly and look closely. I tell them that they better be trying their hardest, because they don't want me to pick a random sample that sucks. I don't tell them that when that happens, I often look around for a better sample. But creative writing class always seemed to yield good lines. I even put it in poetry one day while filling that first blank page with my students:

The Blank Page

What words will I hear
flowing from the young
creative minds who have come
to write in each other's presence?
What languages will
intertwine as each individual
paints their poetic masterpieces
from those first blotches and blurbs
that bubble forth
out of the simmering souls?

Before the term is done
and fades like setting sun,
graceful words written with care
will fill blank pages, lighten the air,
will linger in memoirs, last in song
and rest on full pages where they belong.

Although we wrote many styles and types of creative work during creative writing class, we utilized Olson's lighthearted text as a point of departure for every lesson. *Lighthearted.* That's the trick. And since there was no set curriculum to follow, and since there were no eyes or expectations for the course's outcome (modern administrators and educational experts take note), magic happened. We wrote a poem every day, all of us. We also wrote stories, essays, and other types of prose. And as we worked through Olson's text, we created enough great work to make an in-house literary magazine for every trimester the class was held—30 copies printed on and bound at school as a memento that was momentous to many students and their parents. We titled the literary magazine *At the Summit* for South Summit High School. Each trimester class named their edition with a subtitle. The first year was *Flowing Words and Intertwining Language.* Another was entitled *Changing Villages Amidst Roaming Mountains.* In the interest of the vivid verb, each subtitle *had* to focus on participles.

It was during this time that I also employed one of my favorite techniques for getting reluctant writers to compose poems—the classic acrostic poetry assignment. This trick still works for reticent writers and I use it often. Superstition at Halloween is one of my favorites. Here's a light-hearted example followed by a thought-provoking allusion-filled example I penned for one year's Thanksgiving assignment:

The turkey never
Had a chance between being
All dressed up for the holidays,
Never suspecting that things would
Keep going as status quo, but rather
Soon, in the scope of things, life would inevitably
Go awry for him.
Instead of eating grain and gobbling, his
Very essence was destined for the sharp
Incisions of evil knife after feeling momentarily the
Never ending flames. And his doorway now posts,
Gone For The Season.

Thanatopsis greets us all in spirit when we
Hear the preternatural call, summoning
All reminisce in thankful bliss, remembering those

No longer more than just an ethereal ghost or a
Knell upon some subconscious inward bell.
Shores of pastoral bliss may indeed await those who
Go from loving headlands
Into Emily's eternity.
Veering flaws of Wordsworth's foolish captain who
In "midnight and snow" helps us remember fondly and
Not forget those who have been called forth into "that
Good night."

I only taught creative writing for two years. Demands for elective courses in technology, finance, child development and other politically mandated subjects sliced into the numbers of kids who would sign up for the course like a hungry driver eating pie at a truck stop. As I look back on this time, I realize now that no-one ever asked me if I thought one needed to *be* a creative writer in order to successfully *teach* creative writing. If anyone ever does ask, I think I'll explain that any good writing or English teacher can teach a creative writing course, but only a true writer can *live* such a class—and *living* for something is much more enjoyable than simply doing it *for a living*. Consequently, I faced off with the blank page along with my students; I wrote as much as and sometimes even more than what I expected of them. And while I created a classroom focus of showing off and applauding their work, I often included segments of my own writing for examples. At first, I worried that I might intimidate them with my years of creative practice; then I realized that some of them would intimidate me with their youth, wit, skill, flexibility, and cleverness. One day after my brightest student produced a villanelle that put my simple sonnets to shame and astonished all of us, I elicited class laughter by quoting my long-ago departed friend Bill Turk and said, "Just remember, old age and treachery will overcome youth and skill!" But I'll always remember that villanelle and many of the other pieces that young writer turned out. His name was Rob Mason. I must also explain that many of the essays in this book were born from ideas I came up with while writing with my students. My Frank and Stoney story and "Singing Rainbow," for instance, are two of them. There are perhaps two dozen others that I haven't revised yet, maybe waiting for another book, or maybe ready to make this one longer.

One day, while teaching students a segment from Olson's book on finding ideas with elements of surprise and unique perspective in them, I penned these words for myself and for my students. I distinctly recalled recently losing a long and detailed word document on the computer due to a power blip earlier in the week. Autosave was not part of my word processing system back then. This is what came out:

Writing From BC

I once lived and thrived in the year of one thousand nine hundred and seventy-six B.C, yet that significant date was not so ancient as my words imply. B.C. merely stands for before computers! A great children's poet once pontificated that I should never forget how to write by hand, digitally, on paper, with pencil, or pen. I chuckle now, in the year 2003 A.D. (After Digital) and sometimes write with pen and paper just to enjoy the simple process of sculpting words stylistically, letting the inky images of my brain spill through my dripping, scribbling pen onto lined paper. And I relish most of all that moment, when unsatisfied by my writing results, I can raucously crumple my page and toss it in a perfect arc into the trash—deleted, done—but by choice—not by electronic accident! And I even got to see it go!

My current IB and English teaching load prevents me from teaching electives now, but recently as an English department we lobbied for and won a place for a creative writing class. I encourage everyone to take the course, and even though I know that times and contexts from when I taught the course to now are as different as house cats to mountain lions, the process of learning creativity is immensely important to our world of education. Technology might be the vehicle that drives our world now, but creativity is the fuel that powers it. Music, art, writing, dance, and creative expression counterbalance all the hard sciences. Denying creativity is like denying that humanity comes from and depends upon nature—and that becomes a problematic pathway. I feel lucky to have been able to contribute to creativity in teaching. It's my way of helping humanity direct its own evolution in a positive way.

Chapter 17: A Philosophical Outlook

Every fall on the Autumnal Equinox I take half a dozen eggs to class and balance them on end. I let a few non-believers tip them over, and then let them balance the same eggs. Some years we leave the eggs balanced for hours, even days after the equinox until the shifting balances of earth and seasons compel them to fall over. Some people claim one can balance an egg any time of year. They might be right. But I enjoy creating the lesson related to the balance between night and day, summer and winter. Some years I balance eggs on the Vernal Equinox as well, but the balancing window seems narrower, the task a bit harder. It's best in autumn.

Classroom teaching that works, that has an impact, is a bit like balancing those eggs. It takes such a subtle touch of technique, and above all a belief in the possible.

Classroom teaching in the arena of public education in Utah, and I suspect in other places as well, is like being asked to balance eggs daily—and none of the days are the equinox. Administrators and politicians are moving inexorably in the direction of business models and prescribed curriculum for public education. Teachers are not only being told what to teach, but they are being told how to teach, and even when to teach. Spontaneity and capturing the classic "teaching moment" are becoming casualties of politics and business in education. Creativity is also becoming a casualty. Administrators just can't seem to grasp the concept that creative teaching does not mean loss of content, rigor, or discipline. They do not grasp the idea that creative teaching is a labor of love. A labor of love is by nature disciplined and self-willed. It is a higher form of discipline and will have much more impact than any forced or directed discipline.

A large part of my own creative impetus is driven by nature and a desire to teach conservation—not environmentalism mind you—but conservation, wise use, sustainability, even resilience. I began thinking about teaching the precepts of conservation while using some of the 1970's and 1980's language arts textbooks which featured stories like William Faulkner's *The Bear*, essays like Rachel Carson's *The Edge of the Sea*, and long and thoughtful excerpts from Henry David Thoreau's *Walden.* But I wanted to share more ideas with my students, like those of Aldo Leopold, Rachel Carson, and John Muir, or more contemporary authors like Wallace Stegner, John McFee, Edward Abbey, and Terry Tempest Williams. Williams is another thoughtful conservationist I was lucky enough to perform with on several occasions. And so in the interest of teaching what I love and know, I devote time to writing and sharing stories like the following fable. Instead of grinding through district and state-generated objectives and timelines, I take and make time for stories—stories with lessons in them, stories that inspire students to think, learn, and even read.

Let me introduce one of those stories: Opening a conversation about conservation and the health of wild lands is sometimes like trying to explain a computer to a manual typewriter. Aldo Leopold tells us that the complex interactions of wildland flora and fauna is much too complex for any individual to completely understand.

The story of wild lands, particularly in America, is a story of history and change. Few can grasp the full myriad of changes leading from the typewriter to the computer; fewer yet can comprehend the complexity of land and its changes. Yet perhaps we can keep the keyboard metaphor in mind while we use those same keys for telling a simple story—a tale told from the perspective of some members of the forest community. The aim for both the metaphor and the story is to make us think historically about changing wild lands and carefully ponder actions the future might hold. I penned this for my students one year as a closing to a unit on conservation. Were they more like humans, this is what three anthropomorphized forest members might say:

A Meeting of Minds, Anthropomorphism in the Forest

A Red Fox, a Great Horned Owl, and a White-Tailed Deer gathered in a moonlit glen deep inside the old growth forest.

The Fox spoke first. "Listen, I'm telling you that this forest is all hunted and grazed out. If I could show you the size of the average mouse I eat compared to when I was a kit, well, you'd see they're scrawny as late summer rosehips and slow as a falling snowflake."

"Hmm," broke in the Deer, "and I'll bet it's because they don't eat as well as they used to. I don't even eat as well as I used to. Why, we have to forage twice as far for the same variety of grasses in our diet, but according to the Old Stag we don't even see half as many different kinds of grasses as we used to."

The Fox replied, "Yes, that would make sense. Even the red twig dogwoods I used to enjoy so much for camouflage are scarcer now. Makes me feel like a Bluejay on a patch of white snow when I think of camouflage disappearing. And there were some bunch grasses that used to be nice hiding, too, but I can't find them anymore."

"Well," said the Deer, "Not that I mean anything by it, but I'm glad you predators are a little easier to see. It makes my life a little safer. But you know the Old Stag keeps telling me that we're all getting weaker and sicker and slower because there aren't any wolves, nor as many big cats, bears, and coyotes. How does he figure that?"

The Owl, who had been sitting silently throughout the duration of the conversation readjusted his perch, shook his wings slightly, and then spoke, his keen eyes drilling right into the hides of both the Fox and the Deer. "You both are astute observers, but you are forgetting the Human factor in this complex equation."

"The Human factor, out here?" asked both the Fox and the Deer. "Why, this is a National Park surrounded by refuge habitat and wilderness. They don't live here, hunt here, and rarely even camp here."

"No," stated the Owl looking around the glen at the shadows cast on the illuminated forest floor by the tall timber surrounding them. "They don't often come here, but their influence is as prevalent as the sun; even when the clouds are around, the sun is still shedding light on the forest."

The Fox turned his head sideways and asked, "What do you mean by that?"

"Yes," said the Deer, "If they're not here much, how come you say they're here influencing us?"

"Well," said the Owl, "Let me put it this way. The Humans hunted the great predators until they were nearly extinct, and they still hunt many of them. And now there are so many humans that they are taking up the habitat predators need for survival. How long has it been since you've heard a Wolf in this forest, seen a Grizzly? What about the Wolverine? How many Mountain Lions are around now?"

"I admit," replied the Fox sitting in a beam of moonlight, tail curled around his paws, "that it has been much quieter since I was a kit. And my father told stories . . ."

"Oh yes," chimed in the Deer tapping her forehoof on the pine duff covered forest floor. "The Old Stag keeps telling us stories as well!"

"Yes, yes, you are both right," continued the Owl, "but what you do not see is that because there are less predators, there are more of your type Miss Deer, there are more of the grazing animals. And there have been so many some years that you've eaten certain grasses to death. They no longer exist around here!"

"Ah," commented the Fox, "So that's why the mice aren't so well fed, it's the Deer's fault."

"Not so hasty Mr. Fox. You're on the other side of the scale. Without so many of the other meat-eating mammals, you've had less competition for food, not to mention there are less creatures who find your young kits unaware and have them for breakfast."

The Fox stood up and circled once nervously. "What is your point, Mr. Owl. I don't like thinking about some Lion eating my kits!"

"No, you wouldn't, that's natural. But because there are so many of you, you've eaten the rodent population down to nothing, even the healthy, quick ones. But you're right, they haven't had as much good stuff to eat due to the Deer and therefore are weaker in general and easier to catch."

"Oh, this sounds so complicated!!" exclaimed the Deer as she lowered herself onto her side, slender legs placed along her flanks.

"Ah, yes, it is complicated, and I haven't even started talking about the worms, the birds, and the soils yet. But let's get back to the predators. You see, the Deer overgrazed, then started to get weak also because food became short. But with fewer predators, the weak deer have had weak deer fawns, and consequently, the whole population has gotten weaker with each new generation."

"But so many deer wander outside of the refuge and get taken by Human hunters every year," said the Fox. The Deer shot him an agitated glance while the Owl answered.

"Yes, true, but predators hunt and cull the weak and sick. Human hunters often take the healthiest of the breeding stock, thereby leaving the herd poorer for it all. Only a Lion, a Bear, or a Wolf will settle for a weak, diseased deer."

"Sure," said the Fox, "because it's so darned hard for them to catch a really healthy buck or doe, and if they get gored, well, it hurts!

"Right," returned the Owl, "You're beginning to understand now."

Far off in the forest, a Nighthawk swooped on an insect, wings growling with a surge of air from the dive. The Coyote Clan began yipping at an unsuspecting Jackrabbit caught out of his den. One lone Lion listened carefully from a high perch, debating the safety of movement. The Owl turned his head nearly around, then back again. "Friends, it's time for me to hunt now. Let's meet tomorrow to discuss the insects and the fires."

"More Human influence I suppose?" asked the Deer.

"Yes," said the Owl, "But before I go, I'll tell you that things may change for the better. Some Humans might be getting wiser."

"Tell us, please," urged the Fox. "We need to hear something hopeful. I always like to start the night's hunt on a hopeful note."

"Well," finished the Owl as he lifted his wings to depart, "Twice now I've seen hikers carrying a very special book with a funny name, A Sand County Almanac. Tomorrow I'll tell you what wonderful things that book by Aldo Leopold was saying!" And then he flew off into the night. Shortly after, the fox padded silently into the forest and the Deer slipped into the shadows. Their nocturne had begun.

We might call this a fable. We might call it a truth. We might call it a story by a teacher with an overactive imagination. I like to think of it as a fable, but then sometimes I'm considered old-fashioned. I still sometimes return to the typewriter, that tool on which the early stories of the American wilderness were written. I also return to the wilderness or at least the vestiges of it that have echoed down through the canyons of human expansion.

When I hear the owl call, however, I wonder if she's calling the names of those who will never return. Grasping my copy of Leopold, I teach his words and pray that her nocturne will never become her elegy.

Sometimes I ask myself, are we really heading in the right direction for our children? Terror, climate change, Hollywood characters as presidents, media propaganda, virtual reality—the list goes on. It's up to us as teachers to bring reality back. But good teaching, the kind that really reaches kids and allows for the type of openness and discussion that young people long for doesn't fit into any formula. I'm not saying that we should abandon the curriculum or the quality lesson planning. Part of teacher education training, for instance, is to learn the essence, structure, and importance of lesson planning. Concepts like anticipatory set, objectives, guided practice, reflection, and closing are indeed important, and every good teacher employs them to varying extents. But all too often administrators gravitate to the latest and greatest trends in educational research by requiring that teachers employ these trends on top of everything else they do and have always done. Add to this that new trends then drive new evaluation requirements, and soon teaching becomes an elaborate show designed to demonstrate what some third-party pedagogical guru has determined as best practices.

There is nothing inherently wrong with new trends like feedback loops, pair shares, explicit vocabulary instruction, outcome-based grading, and many other new educational practices, but all too often these practices drive the teaching in a nearly formulaic fashion. Spontaneity and seizing the teaching moment gets lost. We need to allow creative teachers and teaching to thrive, each in their own unique way. Regarding rigor, something everyone is now calling for, let each teacher develop his/her own rigor, style, technique. This may be non-standard in nature, but it will be quality. The classic adage goes, teach what you know, teach what you love. It's almost cliché, but clichés happen because they are small, essential truths oft-used, oft repeated, oft lived. Let each profession in the business world do their own OJT and certifications and education after students graduate high school. Meanwhile we need to let teachers really teach, and teach from the heart.

In my current school district, we've got a 117-page high-tech laminate, super-glossy, full-color nylon spiral bound manual explaining how to fulfill administrative evaluation demands. It's named Canyons Teacher Effectiveness Support System. Ironically, the acronym, CTESS, has a certain onomatopoeic snake-in-the-grass sound to it. And administrators tell us that if we don't do CTESS by the book, it will come back to bite us. The manual is not all bad. It holds a dozen pages of good teaching practices and ideas. But most of the manual is a highly prescribed system by which teachers are expected to perform and be evaluated. The system for observation alone involves an administrator popping in for a random twenty-minute observation using a twenty-second timer and a chart to record student behavior and teacher to student feedback loops. If your class is reading or working independently, as a teacher you score ineffective on the observation. If you dialogue too long with one student, lecture for any length of time, read out loud, tell a story—ineffective. And that's just one element of the CTESSS Manual. Other elements include a highly complicates system of "proving" that you participate in professional learning communities, "proving" via hard evidence that you are using the newest best practices and that those practices are transferring directly to improved student success. The manual also demands administering a computerized interface that takes literally hours of time to navigate, update, and complete. When I began teaching in rural Utah, good teaching naturally employed best practices, professional learning communities, and evidence of growth—but it was not prescribed, it was more of a holistic progression inherent in quality teaching by teachers who loved what they did. And the observation system was simple, clear and practical. Twice a year, our principal would sit through an entire class from start to finish, which would then be followed up by a post-observation interview. Added to this, the principal would also do three to five "drop-in" visits to each class just to see how things were going. It didn't take a huge manual for an administrator to see how things were going, both the good and the bad, and to compliment the good and to constructively critique the bad. But that was another time.

My current reality is that every year I teach more and more students with less and less time, which means class loads of 190 to 215 students *in English class.* (When 200 students turn in a two-page essay, I have 400 pages to assess.) I'm asked to use an ever-changing array of new technologies, all going online long before I've mastered the old technologies, and we have one part-time technology specialist for over 150 faculty members. We don't have adequate support. Oh, but we do have a 117 page high-tech laminate super glossy full-color nylon spiral bound how to get evaluated manual! Every year, the Mormon Church brings in thousands of refugees, who land in the schools. Hispanic Americans bring their relatives from Mexico and other immigrants come from all over the world, so that any given regular education class has as many as a third of its students classified ESL. We have one part-time ESL coordinator who has to handle as many as twenty different nationalities and languages. And these kids are expected to be taught the regular curriculum at grade level. We don't have a fraction of the help to bring these kids up. Oh, but we have 117 page high-tech laminate super glossy full-color nylon spiral bound how to get evaluated manual! We have drug users, gang members, a boatload of mainstreamed special ed. kids of all sorts, misfits, miscreants, and a world of entitled Whites all crammed into the same forty kids per classroom where we are expected to give quality bell to bell instruction and meet ever more detailed and data-driven curricular demands. We just don't have the ability to accomplish the impossible every day. Oh, but we do have. . .

It's hard to keep a sense of self, a sense of purpose, and, most importantly, a sense of humor throughout all of this. I walk down the hall and stop by a colleague's room for a visit.

"So how did the district meeting for the English Department go?" I ask. I was at the International Baccalaureate meeting which happened at the same time.

"Oh, they heard us, I think. We told them that it's impractical, even impossible for everyone to teach the same thing at the same time in the same way. But we know things won't change."

"Ah, so we just keep doing what we do and spin the data when they want it, the way they want it. Nothing like livin' a lie."

"Yep. I call it making the implausible plausible and possiblizing the impossible."

"You make me laugh, you know that? Thanks!" I move on.

A short time later I run into another faculty member, this time an Art teacher. He shakes his head, "Now they want us to learn Google Drive and the new CTESS and Canvas platforms. Hell, I never got familiar with Dropbox and Google docs, plus they never help with Skyward, Outlook Web, and the old Adobe. And now they want us to use the new Adobe fill-and-send forms, and my laptop can't handle the program." But the CTESS Manual contains absolutely nothing about how to implement and administer even one of the complicated computer systems required for the job. It doesn't even give hints for navigating its own online component!

But every year at school startup, we watch a video from the district and state offices of education explaining the consequences of not meeting evaluation standards. The speaker on the video claims that first, a substandard teacher will be assigned a peer coach to improve their performance. If they don't improve, then they will not have their contract renewed. They should simply say, "You'll receive a pink slip," or better yet, "You'll be fired."

I've spent many a faculty meeting feeling the creativity sucked out of me by mandates that are as useless as wet toilet paper. In a fit of pique, sometimes I'll pen a poem for my colleagues. I call this a cynical or sarcastic catharsis. My colleagues smiled and chuckled at both of these when I presented them. The first, a metaphor for dark times, and the second was written during test season while teachers were being grilled on test mandates, procedures and ethics.

To my uniquely gifted cohorts—Two poems

A Burnt Candle

As I celebrate the Winter Solstice
With a candle that does not,
Burn at both ends,
I think of light returning,
And recall the many times
Our conversations—
Our collusions,
During these wintry times,
Have kindled an extra flame
Within me
For education.

To Size the Test A Sonnet

To test or not to test we ask ourselves,
Although the ones in charge have made our choice,
And so the best of learning becomes shelved
While pressure cooking binds and chokes our voice.
The teaching world that once embodied growth
Was filled with natural spontaneity.
Creative minds of kids and teachers both
Could make true learning seem as fun and free.
To "seize the day" is something all but lost,

The teaching moment boxed and analyzed.
Perhaps we need to reassess the cost
Of proving what we've always realized.
There is a thoughtful, knowing paradigm
To which we are becoming wholly blind.

When I return to my room from my rather eventful walk to the bathroom and mailboxes, which led me to visit with the aforementioned colleagues, I find two students waiting at my door for help. I'm thinking I need to get online and work on that damned CTESS program, but fate has other plans for me right now. One student needs help setting up her phone for translation—she's been in the U.S. for barely four months, the other is there to tell me that his mother is going in for cancer surgery for a malignant tumor. So what is *really* important?

Just being there is really important for most of my students. Maslow would probably agree; administrators simply put on political blinders. Nearly every time I finish class early and give kids a little downtime, one of my students comes to me with a huge problem from home—something that caused them to miss class last time, something that was the reason they were distracted today, something they need to get off their chest. And I think of mandates like making sure that meaningful education is going on from bell to bell and say to hell with it!

I tried to capture this sentiment in poetry one year. Again, I penned this sonnet during another frustrating midyear meeting, just before the holidays.

Acrostic The Halls Sonnet

Most people cannot fully comprehend
Exactly what it is we do for work.
Red ink ostensibly is our best friend,
(Red tape, more like it, and dealing with jerks!)
Yet persevering despite the parent ploys,
Conniving kids, administrative rules,
Half interest, boredom, IPods, cellphone toys,
Reluctant learners and entitled fools.
In spite of all the games, *we still do teach*
So there can be consistency each day
To keep them all aware of how to reach—
Make graduation happen one fine May.
And most will realize when they grow up,
Some people in this world can care like us!

One year a colleague asked me, "Why don't you have your students write their one page *About Me* essays anymore?"

"It's too depressing," I reply. "It's better to let them tell me slowly, throughout the year, when they are ready to unload. But it's a horrible way to start a school year—reading reality."

I could never keep all their stories straight anyway, not without knowing their names and faces. A bunch of introductory essays never worked for me. In my view, just being there requires instructional or educational downtime with students—requires a one-on-one experience with each one in order to learn who they really are, requires alternative type lessons, spur-of-the-moment changes in lesson plans, and, well, quite simply: creativity.

I believe that creativity in teaching, things like metaphors for the classroom, doing artwork occasionally instead of writing paragraphs, listening to and telling stories, and all the other elements of the spontaneous and artistic side of passionate teaching has another important impact: it distracts students from everyday life. And for many, everyday life is not so good. I'll admit that avoiding problems is not the same as coping with them, but as a teacher, I am only marginally equipped to effectively help students learn to cope. When I am able to do so, it's almost always a one-on-one requirement, not something that works during instructional class time. I also consider that the metaphors I use for forests, wilderness, rivers, and the outdoors, which are so prominent in literature, are little known by the average city kid, especially the one who does not read much and does not take advanced classes. So I now need time to craft metaphors that embrace the urban forest, the city park, the irrigation canal, the local reservoir, and even the constellation of city lights seen from hills above town. There are, after all, many interpretations of the concept we call *nature,* just as there are many different ways of reaching students. But I believe that the disconnect of humanity from the natural world is becoming more and more a factor in social illness. Even if I can bring little pieces of the natural world to education, I believe that those little pieces can keep the often tenuous connection between man and nature alive. Perhaps I should go back to guiding full time, maybe even take groups of students out for multi-day trips in the outdoors. I very nearly went that route early on, but the pay was horrible and the season short. So I settle for the sparks that will ignite the passion for a world beyond the computer or phone screen. Many of my students are someday going to want peace in the midst of man-made noise and chaos. Suddenly one day they will be sitting at a bus stop and hear a bird sing and want more. They might learn to care for birds more than they care for mosquito-free parks. They will see a geranium blooming on a counter in the south facing winter sun and want that as well. They will want parks and open spaces more than they want new shopping malls. They will hear and smell the rain, then feel the silence of the fog, and one day maybe even discern the subtle sound of snowflakes falling. When that happens, they might remember authors like Carson, Gore, Wilson, Thoreau, Muir, Abbey, Leopold, Williams, McPhee, Stegner and others. Some might even remember those crazy writing topics way back in high school English class, and they will wonder.

Maybe it's my own love for escaping reality that drives my impulse for classroom creativity. Stories, poems, novels, even essays, can all do this. So can art, objects, and music. For me personally, the reality of nature as an antithesis to society does wonders for the mind and imagination. That's why these are the elements that drive my teaching; they are elements that make up the objects in my room and the subjects for my voice that I share with young minds. I don't force the concept of the imbalance between man and nature. I just live for nature and let the students figure out for themselves that there is such a thing as balance—that there are often imbalances. Of course, authors like Aldo Leopold and Rachel Carson give the ethos to my essence.

Much has changed in education during the past thirty years, and I have adapted to much of that change. I incorporate new pedagogical concepts when I see their merit, but I do it in my own time and through my own devices. I just won't sacrifice that creativity and spontaneity to match the newest trend in educational practices. One day, after working to adapt the Pre-During-Post note-taking strategy into text readings, I thought to myself, *At what point does too much transformation occur? I have transformed constantly in my teaching to fulfill the demands of administrators and political processes in education. Each transformation results in a loss of some of the real essence of teaching. When asking students to draw or sketch, I see many stick figures and emojis where I once saw more creative sketches by students. As for myself, I write on a whiteboard now rather than on a chalkboard, and sketching is much more limited. But the biggest factor is the loss of reading time due to the increase of gaming, texting, and social media time. Even the textbooks have changed for the worse. They used to be organized neatly by genres, or by chronological order of history and literature. Now they have all kinds of genres and excerpts all mashed together into thematic units. Don't get me wrong, interdisciplinary units are wonderful, but they are best when put together by the individual teacher rather than a distant person who chooses the unit theme and which texts they as editors feel the unit needs. Part of the joy of putting together interdisciplinary units is the learning we as educators gain while we think and read and research and plan. And doing this during the teaching process with students exploring alongside educators is so much more powerful than accessing a textbook where it's all done for you, and sometimes not all of it is interesting to either you or the students. I want to name my own themes, not have some distant textbook writer and editorial staff do it for me.* Piqued, slightly frustrated, I fought back once again. I added boxes for artwork on the PDP notes I was preparing and created a segment for a short poem to be included. Finally, I scrawled EDDY as an acronym on top where the classic objective was to be included. What does EDDY stand for? Engage, Discover, Delight, Yearn.

The door to my classroom greets students with a paper cutout of mountains. Green below, then purple, dark blue, light blue, and finally white on top. The foreground of the mountains hosts a verse from a song by Dan Fogelberg:

The higher you climb,
The more that you see.
The more that you see,
The less that you know.
The less that you know,
The more that you yearn.
The more that you yearn,
The higher you climb.

At the end of the year, it's the last starter song I play for my students. Teaching, in reality, is a hell of a lot of hard work. But when it's done out of passion and love, it comes with a special set of rewards, a special feeling of fulfillment and accomplishment.

It does, however, take some prescience to see that accomplishment. For example, what about the kid who sits in a class all year long, never does a lick of work, responds minimally to any question, query, or individual attention, and fails the class? I've had these kids return years later after finishing their high school diploma through alternative programs or online systems to tell me that they learned more in my class than any other class they ever took. What the hell? How did that happen? In time, I realized that though they never wrote more than fifty words down on paper, even though they never participated in a single discussion, even though they never handed in a lick of work, even though they seemed like they were sleeping most of the time, they were there. They were present. They absorbed everything I taught during the year, and perhaps they digested the information and truly critically analyzed it, thought about it, even sought out more knowledge in their own way. Some of these kids, who I used to consider not only failures but *my failures,* actually have become more successful than the A students. So how does an administrator evaluate *that* type of success? How do I evaluate *that* type of success? After many long years, I have found a way to at least believe in and hope for that type of success. My conviction that even a failing, lump-on-a-log type student can and often does learn and grow compels me to stay the course, to keep creativity alive. It compels me to teach with passion and teach with the knowledge that, even if it looks like only one or two students are engaged and with me at any given time, there is an entire silent audience soaking up knowledge like a tree on a dewy morning during a drought. And what do I do when tasked to perform "evidence-based learning?" For now, I spin the results as much as possible in favor of the A students. Someday when I'm forced to account for not being able to get results from the non-participating students, I'll simply play my last cards. It's a drawer crammed full of cards and letters and thank-yous from students—many of them once considered failures.

You see, in my mind, a good classroom is not solely a place where grades are made, but it is a place where young minds and personalities are given opportunity to grow, even if that growth is wild and crazy and unmeasurable. It's a home, a place for hope and comfort and the ability to make mistakes and learn from them, and even a place sometimes just to rest. On a good day it's also a place to dream.

"Ok everyone, let's dream for a moment. Let's imagine. What would it be like to write a letter using a feather quill pen and an inkwell filled with ink made from local berries?"

I see bemused looks. I take the long feather from its pushpin holders on the bulletin board and wave it around in the air like I'm writing. I dip it into an imaginary inkwell. Then I blow on an imaginary paper to dry the ink.

"Can you imagine ironing clothes with this?" I hold up the solid hunk of iron with the 5 lb. mark stamped in it and the slender handle cast to hold it. "This old iron doesn't even have a coil of metal around the handle to protect your hand. You'd have to use a cloth or a glove. And your wood-stove would have to be pretty hot, wouldn't it?"

I hold the antique iron as if I'm ironing a pair of pants in front of me, then hold them up while I place the iron back on the writing topic bookshelf top.

"It's the end of World War II. You live on a remote farm in Oklahoma, twenty miles from town. Coming in from work, you hear the news on this transistor radio, which is the only link you have to the outside world. And when night falls, you hear more reports from stations even farther away, because the signals bounce off the ionosphere and are not impeded by the electromagnetic interference from the sun. What a story."

While talking, I telescope the radio's antenna and hold it up to my ear, turning the dials. I collapse the antenna and place the radio back in its place on the shelf.

"Which character in Twain's *Huckleberry Finn* made Huck a new leather hat after he lost his old one in the Mississippi River? Did Huck ever run into a beaver trapper or a flamingo hunter during his travels? What would he say if he knew that hat styles were causing the demise and near extinction of the beaver, the otter, the flamingo?"

I wave the old leather hat over the Audubon Field Guide and hang it on its bulletin board hook.

The school year is near its end. Within a few days, I'll pack up all the writing topics and store them away until next year. Within ten years or less, I'll pack up the rest of the classroom and let in the younger generation of teachers. Like a sketch on an old chalkboard, my time will be erased, the chalkboard itself replaced by new technology and new paradigms of business and education. But *my* memory will remain filled with songs, stories, poems, and physical objects that helped create the early imagination-filled classrooms in rural Utah, and later Café 22, the C-211 Wilderness, and the A-203 Eddy. It was the natural world and creativity that kept me going year after year in a job that might have been mundane but never was; perhaps that force of imagination will continue, like a wave crossing endlessly changing waters.

Epilogue

Using a little imagination, I've extrapolated on actual words, phrases, and comments I've heard over the years from both students and parents. These dialogues might be a bit more formal sounding than hallway talk, but the essence remains.

Tanya

"What did you learn in English today Tanya?"

"Oh, Doherty's class. He's uh, kinda different."

"Different?"

"Yeah. First, we listen to some old hokey folk song and have to write about it. He locks the door, too, so if you're late you don't get points. He says it's so he won't get distracted and forget the words, but I think he likes shutting some people out."

"I see. You said that he might forget the words. Does he actually sing the songs?"

"Yeah, and he plays the guitar with it. It's actually kinda nice, like that coffee house concert you and Dad took me to last year up at the college."

"What song did he play today?"

"It was this long song about railroads by a guy named Gordon."

"Gordon Lightfoot?"

"Yeah, that's him. Doherty said it was the history of the railroads and western expansion all done in a poem. How does he remember all those words?"

"Well, honey, he's probably spent a lot of time on it. So what did you do after the song?"

"Then he got all dramatic and said he'd have to dig around in a box in a cabinet to choose a new writing topic. Then he pulled out a stupid hunk of firewood and we had to write about it. First, we had to write all about a feather. Now it's a piece of a tree."

"That sounds better than doing a diary or a journal, doesn't it? You hated doing those journals last year, and the one in seventh grade. Tell me more about what you write for Mr. Doherty."

"Don't remind me about that seventh-grade class! So we just talked about trees as a resource, then wrote a page on our ideas. But next class he says we're going to get technical and write on something he calls, um lemme think. . . oh yes, dendrochronology. He said dendro means tree and chrono means time. He calls day two of writing the technical day. Then we write a poem on day three, a story on day four, and some silly dialogue on day five and we're done with that topic."

"That sounds pretty interesting, Tanya. What do you do after writing?"

"Oh, I almost forgot, we read for fifteen minutes first each day. He calls it our meditation time, says he can hear the words falling like snowflakes into our brains. I think he's a bit nuts sometimes. But after writing then we do a silly little grammar lesson. He picks one vocabulary word for each day and raves about it, then we talk grammar. Today we did a little lesson on abstract nouns. Boring."

"Well, honey, it *is* English."

"No, Mom, it's the Eddy."

"The Eddy?"

"Yeah, he calls our class The Eddy. Every darned day he talks about rivers and eddies and says that we've "eddied out" for a while and have time to look closely at things like swabats."

"Swabats?"

"Students will all be able to do this or do that."

"Oh."

"It's his nickname for objectives. Yeah, I know. It's kinda stupid. He says the swabats are furry little creatures that can be seen on the riverbank when we're all eddied out. And rope. He uses rope for his rules: respect, on time, prepared, and excellence."

"Sounds reasonable. So, do you like the class? It seems like you know quite a bit about it already."

"I guess it's ok. He took a point off my last PDP notes though because I didn't write in complete sentences."

"Well, you know how to write in complete sentences."

"I know. We're going to write a big old essay next week. He says we can make up lost points on that one if we do a good job."

"What's the essay going to be about?"

"We have to analyze the impact of Indian cultures on American Literature. He calls them First People cultures. We've been reading bits and pieces, like Native mythology, a few novel chapters, some other stuff."

"Hmm, that sounds like a good challenge. Can you remember some of the novels?"

"One was about an owl,"

"*I Heard the Owl Call My Name* by Margaret Craven?"

"Yeah, that's one of them."

"Tanya, that's one of my favorite books! See, it's here on the top shelf! Are you going to read it as a class?"

"I don't think so, but he said something about it being one of the optional titles for next semester."

"Well, choose it if you can. We'll read it together!"

"All right, Mom. I'll give it a try."

"Well, Mr. Doherty sounds like he's quite different for an English teacher."

"Oh, he's different all right. I just hope he's not stingy with his grades."

"Well, Tanya, you could have taken the AP English this year. If you think of how hard that would have been, I'll bet you'll be ok."

"I hope so. I'm just glad I'm not in his IB class. He keeps saying that they run more rapids than we do. I think that means that the class is a lot harder."

James

"James, how is your IB English course coming along?"

"I'm getting an A right now Dad. It's going ok."

"Can you tell me what you're studying?"

"Yeah, we're doing a unit on conservation authors which is designed to get us ready for the big IB essay on text analysis, mostly stuff on rhetoric and rhetorical devices."

"Is he an environmentalist?"

"Naw, I don't think so. But he does ride his bike to school nearly every day. He says his ideas come from Thoreau and that summer read author I had to read, Aldo Leopold. He claims that the word *environmentalist* wasn't even in the dictionary until after Rachel Carson wrote and that he's a conservationist.

"Aldo Leopold? Hmm, do you still have a copy of that book? I might have to read it."

"Yeah, Dad, it's on the library shelf. You might like it a lot more than me. It's got a lot of old history in it—lots of stuff I didn't understand. But we're going through some of it again this year in Doherty's class."

"How is Mr. Doherty as a teacher?"

"He really seems to like to teach. He even sings us a song every day and we have to think like hell about it. Have to write on its theme, its essence, its poetic devices, and then we even have to create a theory of knowledge question for the poem. It's made me listen to song lyrics in a different way."

"What kind of songs does he use?"

"Mostly 60's, 70's, and 80's folk music. He says that was the peak of American lyrical poetry with social impact. Today he did a song by John Prine called "Hello in There." Really made us think.

"I know John Prine. I think I remember that song. He's one of your grandfather's favorites. I'll bet grandpa still has some old vinyl of Prine."

"Wow, I'll have to ask him next time we visit. Maybe he has some Gordon Lightfoot or Kate Wolf also."

"Son, I think your mother has Gordon Lightfoot albums. You should ask her."

"Really?"

"Really. It's one reason we kept that old stereo system up in the den. So tell me more about English class."

"Well, I think Mr. Doherty's class will get me pretty well prepared for my IB finals this year. He doesn't have anywhere near enough time to read all our writing, but when he does read something, he gives us great feedback. And if we get any topics related to nature or conservation, well, we'll all do really great essays."

Charlie

"Charles, If you don't fly straight, I'm going to send you to your father. If you think Utah was not your style, wait until you try North Dakota!"

"Hey, Mom. School's just not my thing. I'd rather get a job."

"A job. Like my job? Night shift, sixty hours a week? Do you really want that?"

"No, Mom, not like yours."

"Then why did I get an email from your English teacher. What's up? You *walked out of class early* three times in a row? And you didn't ask permission or anything?"

"I had to get out. Frank and Joe were after me, said they'd beat the piss out of me after school."

"Oh, Charlie. Why can't you choose better people to be around? But you've been going to English class."

"Yeah, the dude that teaches English is actually kinda interesting."

"But you're failing the class."

"Yeah, I just don't do any of the work. But I get a lot out of the class. He has some neat ideas and changes things up a lot. It's never dull."

"Charlie, you just need to get through high school. When you turn eighteen, you can go to work full time, but you really need to graduate. Do you think your English teacher, uh, what's his name?"

"Mr. Doherty."

"Do you think Mr. Doherty is angry with you? Does he have anything against you?"

"No, Mom. He even asked me about my leaving early, said he was sorry but had to mark me absent. Said something about liability. Said he wished I'd stick around."

"Well, he sounds reasonable. You got these three absences marked against you, but you don't have any tardies for his class. You're the king of tardies, why not his class?"

"Don't go there, Mom. He locks the door if we're late."

"Locks the door? Doesn't he open it when students come?"

"Yeah, but not until after the song."

"After the song?"

"It's how he starts class, with a song. I hate to miss his songs."

"Then *talk* to him, Charlie. Stay in class. Stay in school. Do it for yourself, not for me. Just know this, you will always be glad you finished. And that you'll have to trust me on."

"Ok, Mom. I'll try."

I know that my unconventional and often creative methods make a difference. For one thing, they make my own life as a teacher much more enjoyable. But I also like to think of creativity as rain, it nourishes. When rain falls in the forest, some drops linger on the needles and leaves, shining like gemstones before they seek the rich, loamy earth. Other drops sink quickly and deeply into the soil, nurturing the roots. And a few diffuse into the air to become the misty fog that rolls through the trees and hills and blankets the world with humidity. But when rain falls in the forest, no drop is wasted or lost. I like to think of moments spent teaching as raindrops. If rain is life, then teaching and learning are life's roots, thriving on the rain.

About the Author

When long-time outdoorsman, songwriter, and poet Mark Doherty decided he needed a stable profession for his day job in the 1990's, he began his career as a high school teacher. But Doherty never really left the outdoors and his music behind; he just incorporated them into his creative approach to teaching high school English and writing. After earning his BA in English and Writing from his home state of Colorado at Western State University, Doherty spent ten years working as a musician, backcountry guide, and freelance writer in Southern Utah. Later he earned a teaching degree from Westminster College in Salt Lake City and now teaches International Baccalaureate Senior English as well as 11th grade core English in Midvale, Utah, a suburb of Salt Lake City located at the foot of the Wasatch Mountain Range. He earned his master's degree in Writing Nonfiction from Southern New Hampshire University in November of 2016.

To learn more about Mark's writing and music, visit his website: www.moenkopimemories.org

About the Press

Unsolicited Press is based in Portland, Oregon. The small press is operated by hard-working volunteers who believe books are art and should be spread without discretion. Unsolicited Press publishes new and award-winning authors of poetry, fiction, and nonfiction.

Learn more at www.unsolicitedpress.com.

www.ingramcontent.com/pod-product-compliance
Lightning Source LLC
Chambersburg PA
CBHW050358190726
48284CB00007BB/2344

9781950730025